THE
HISTORY
OF
LACE

THE
HISTORY
OF
LACE

Margaret Simeon

Stainer & Bell: London

© 1979 Illustrations and text Margaret Simeon

All rights reserved. No part of this publication may be reproduced, stored in a retrieval system, or transmitted, in any form or by any means, electronic, mechanical, photocopying, or otherwise, without the prior permission of Stainer and Bell Ltd, 82 High Road, East Finchley, London N2 9PW.

ISBN 0 85249 445 9

Set in Monophoto Ehrhardt by
Butler & Tanner Ltd, Frome and London

Production and design services by Elron Press Ltd, 20 Garrick Street, London WC2.

Title page illustration: an example of unfinished work on a seventeenth century lace sampler.

A piece of folded parchment, still faintly showing the lettering of an old document written on the other side, has been tacked behind the linen to support the cut-work. The narrow vertical and horizontal bands on which the lace-worker was constructing the reticella are made from small groups of threads of the original weaving left in position and worked over with figure of eight stitches. Double threads, added to support the curved lines of the design, are held in position by being couched down on to the parchment. If the work had been completed, these couching stitches would have been cut, from the back, to release the lace. The design itself is built of rows of buttonhole stitches.

The fine needle, still threaded, is pinned into the linen as it was left by the lace-worker over three hundred years ago.

To the memory of my mother and our happy days collecting lace

Contents

List of Plates

Preface

Acknowledgements

I have written this book because I have come to love antique lace through collecting and handling it for nearly forty years, and have become familiar with the changing styles and the great beauty of its design. The lace that has been photographed for these plates is from my own collection, and naturally includes some of my most cherished pieces, but I have tried also to give typical specimens right through its history.

In the second half of the sixteenth century, the early part of this history, designs, although very attractive, were necessarily simple. The greater skill of the lace-workers during the seventeenth and later centuries made it possible for them to use richer and more freely drawn designs in the baroque, rococo and later styles of the succeeding periods. Little masterpieces of design can be found amongst them, worthy of far more careful study than they usually receive.

Perhaps the very charm and delicacy of lace, and the almost unbelievable patience and technical skill required by the workers, has led to the appreciation of the craft taking precedence over that of the art, but truly they must go hand in hand. What the lace-makers and the designers created together is the work of art.

MARGARET SIMEON
1978

I wish to thank Ronald E. Brown and Gerald Howson most sincerely for their skill and patience in producing the fine photographs of my lace, reproduced for the plates of this book. Gerald Howson took those for Plates 12, 45, 57, 63, 98 and 132a, and Ronald Brown took all the rest, a truly monumental task.

I am also most grateful to my sister Eunice for the long and tedious hours she has spent checking typing and proofs, at the various stages of production.

I. Lace-makers and Designers and their Patrons

The plates in this book show the development of the design of hand-made lace from its beginnings in the sixteenth century to the late nineteenth century, as well as giving, I hope, some feeling of its beautiful texture and delicacy.

Design in any craft expresses the tastes and wishes of its patrons, and alters with the changing conditions of society, so this development is just part of the whole history of decoration in Europe throughout the period. If a particular group of designs were out of step or out of sympathy with others of the same time, the goods made from them would be unacceptable. In any case, designers working under similar conditions are consciously or subconsciously influenced by the prevalent taste and by each other's work.

Fine lace was always a luxury, very expensive because of the great time needed for its production. It could in fact be the most costly part of dress, both for men and women, rivalling or surpassing in value that of the jewellery worn; so, at its best, it is a reflection of the sophisticated taste of the aristocracy. The most desired lace was superbly made, of the finest thread available, and beautifully designed by professional artists in the fashion of its time. Fashion in lace was to a considerable extent international, as its lightness and high value made it ideal for trade. The wealthy of every country in Europe would wish to wear the particular type of lace that was considered the most exquisite at the time and

had been made in the town or country that then led the fashion. These great centres of lace-making, at first in Italy and then in France and Flanders, set the style, and their exports were copied, with more or less success, for those who could not afford the very finest. There were certain national variations of technique and design which will be described later.

Import restrictions and prohibitions interfered with the trade quite often when the governments of various countries became alarmed at the enormous amount of money being spent on foreign lace. Like all sumptuary laws, the restrictions had little permanent effect. They were often flouted even at the royal courts, and the smuggling of lace was widespread.

Apart from artistic fashion, the materials and techniques of any craft have great influence on its design. This influence is especially strong in early periods, and always becomes less obvious as craftsmen attain greater skill. In the case of lace, it was during the sixteenth century that the influence of the square mesh of cloth made geometric designs predominant (Plates 11 and 13). Development of skill was particularly swift, and even by the early seventeenth century some lace-makers were able to free themselves from this restraint and use flowing lines in their work (Plate 16). By the mid seventeenth century lace design was in no way less sophisticated than that of crafts established hundreds of years earlier, such as embroidery or decorative wood carving.

Lace-makers who produced the aristocratic laces learned the craft in childhood, in lace schools or in convents or from their parents, and had to continue to work exclusively in this trade to acquire their astonishing skill and keep their hands sufficiently delicate and sensitive to handle the gossamer-fine thread used for the best lace. They were fully professional. Workers whose sight had deteriorated, or who never attained the greatest skill, made coarser and simpler lace for the less wealthy. The great majority of lace-makers were women, but there have always been some men in the craft, particularly in the earlier centuries.

A common system of producing lace was for a lace dealer, a person of substance, to provide the workers with linen thread and parchment patterns for the lace he wanted, collect the finished lace, and pay for the work done. The workers were modestly paid, as were most craftsmen during the same periods, but the lace dealers could make considerable profits. Fine linen thread was itself very costly, and by this arrangement the workers did not have to buy it. Also, drawing the designs on parchment, specially the more elaborate ones, was a skilled job for which the ordinary lace-maker was not trained. Sometimes it is only too evident that a piece of lace has been made on a badly drawn design; what were intended to be fine scrolling forms have degenerated into jerky and disjointed lines, and even when the actual lace-work is good, the effect has been ruined.

In prosperous centres of the craft, production was at times organized on a larger scale. Work was divided up, with specialists doing the different parts. During the eighteenth century a great quantity of very fine lace was made in Brussels, where some workers made the motifs of the pattern, some the ground mesh called the *réseau*, others the elaborate diaper patterns called 'fillings', *à jours* or *modes*, the sole task of others was to join the sections together.

For many centuries it has been fashionable for ladies to do needlework, partly as useful work, but partly for recreation. They have also made lace for their own use, but to produce the finest was too laborious for all but a few. This amateur work was mainly for the decoration of household linen in the earlier part of the history of lace. Although often fine by modern standards, it is usually considerably coarser than that worn on costume at the same time. On the other hand, much good lace was made in convents, often for church use, but also for sale.

Peasant lace has always differed greatly from the fine lace of fashion. It was usually fairly narrow and always of simple, often geometric design that hardly changed over long periods, and was made with much coarser thread. The workers therefore needed neither great skill, nor to keep their hands soft and delicate. Some peasant lace was made professionally and sold by pedlars and at fairs, but it could also be made in spare time after the day's work. Even so, it was seldom used on working clothes, but rather on 'Sunday best' or on the traditional peasant dress of the district.

II. Early Lace – The Sixteenth and Early Seventeenth Centuries

Lace-making is almost wholly a European craft. The drawn thread embroidery, from which one sort of lace was derived, may be Saracenic in origin, but it had been adopted by European embroiderers long before any real lace was produced.

From the sixteenth century there have always been two basic methods. One type of lace was made with a needle and thread; it developed from embroidery and used some of the embroidery stitches. This is known as needlepoint lace: *point*, from the French, meaning 'stitch'. The other was made by twisting and plaiting threads around and between pins that controlled the design. This is called bobbin lace, as the threads were carried on bobbins, or sometimes pillow lace, because the work was always done over a hard pillow. The latter is not a good name, as the makers of needlepoint lace sometimes also used a pillow to support their work, although for them it was not essential. Bobbin lace probably developed from the making of fancy braids and cords which in the fifteenth century were used to decorate and lace up costume. These even then were called 'laces', a word derived from the Latin *laqueus*, meaning a loop or noose. Later it also came to mean the openwork fabric we now call lace, whether made with bobbins or the needle. In the sixteenth century the word *passement* was sometimes used for lace, and *passement dentelé*, in France, for lace with the typical pointed or toothed edge that was so fashionable on collars and ruffs. By the late sixteenth century the French were using simply *dentelle* for any kind of lace, and have done so ever since.

In each chapter of this book, the needlepoint lace of the period will be described first, and then the bobbin lace. The designs for both were quite closely related. Usually needlepoint was more expensive than bobbin lace of comparable fineness, as the process was on the whole slower, but it cannot be said as a generalization that needlepoint is better than bobbin-made. Each has its own beauty.

Needlepoint is firm and crisp, and its design is very clear and sharply defined. This comes from the close needlework, mostly in buttonhole stitching, where a little pull is given to every separate stitch as it is made. Bobbin lace has a soft, lissom quality that makes it extraordinarily graceful, and when gathered it hangs beautifully in soft folds. These particular qualities suited the tastes of different centuries, so each type had its own periods of prominence. During the sixteenth and seventeenth centuries fashion demanded that lace, like the silks and velvets of the time, should be magnificent, and it was worn spread nearly flatly to show all the detail of its splendid bold designs. Needlepoint lace by its very nature was firm and clear and could give all the glorious richness that was desired. Bobbin lace-makers of this period obviously copied the designs of needlepoint, and the Italians in particular worked their lace as tightly as possible to imitate its strength. Flemish bobbin work always tended to be more open in texture.

Gradually, near the end of the seventeenth century, the patterns were reduced in scale; the lace became lighter and began to be worn slightly gathered. As the eighteenth century proceeded the whole fashion of design turned towards delicacy. Lace was no longer grand but deliciously elegant and dainty. Bobbin lace could express this mood perfectly, and in unbelievably fine ruffles and flounces quite equalled the needle-made lace. During the eighteenth century the design of both was a development from seventeenth century bobbin lace rather than from needlepoint.

Needlepoint Lace

In the Gothic period embroiderers sometimes decorated linen for the church, or for domestic furnishings, by drawing out threads, or cutting away small parts of the fabric and working patterns in the spaces. Both processes can be classed as beginnings of lace, as they produce a solid pattern on an open background. They were used more frequently in the sixteenth century, and became popular for the decoration of linen shirts, for both men and women.

Plate 1 shows part of a drawn thread panel, with the groups of remaining threads whipped over and the solid pattern darned in again. Plate 2 illustrates a variation of this technique. The

Plate 1 Drawn Thread Work, Italian. The design is darned back into the drawn thread mesh. Late sixteenth century. Width 22 cm.

Plate 2 Drawn Thread Work, with the design left in the original weaving. Late sixteenth or early seventeenth century. Width 21 cm.

threads were only withdrawn from the background, leaving the pattern in the original weaving. The background threads were whipped over as before, and in this case also the edges of the pattern, to prevent the cut threads from fraying.

Knotted netting, like small-scale fish net, was also used as a ground for darned work (Plates 3, 4 and 5). This is called *lacis* or *filet*. It shows the design more sharply than drawn thread, as the netting is more open and so gives a stronger contrast. In Plate 4*a* the pattern has been worked partly in linen and partly in coloured silks, using a fancy filling as well as darning. *Buratto* is similar to lacis, the only difference being in the net foundation. In buratto this was made by twisting instead of knotting the threads (Plate 7).

These early designs are quite adventurous, if somewhat primitive. The square mesh controls the lines and gives very angular drawing, but they show lively invention and often a sense of fun. The thread is not very fine, but the work is usually even and skilful. Similar pieces were produced in the sixteenth and seventeenth centuries, and in different countries. It is not always possible to be sure where a particular specimen was made. The more sophisticated designs of those in Plate 4 strongly suggest Italy, which was then artistically the leading country in Europe. During the sixteenth and until late in the seventeenth century, the needlepoint laces of Italy, and especially of Venice, were supreme in the quality of their design and workmanship.

Variations of the chequered pattern of the cover in Plate 3 were used very frequently for furnishings. This one is made of large squares of lacis alternating with simple embroidered linen. The tiny geometric squares between them

Plate 3   Cover of Lacis and Cut Work, Italian. Late sixteenth century. Width 72 cm; complete length 168 cm.

are joined only by the corners, so the whole cover is very loosely constructed. Plate 6 shows another of the same type, but with the edges of all the squares sewn together, which is more usual. The lacis here is more elaborate, and the netting is nearly hidden by the designs worked on it. A rather later example of lacis, from the seventeenth century, is shown on Plate 8; the design has been outlined to draw the curves more smoothly. This piece is probably German work.

Linen clothing of the first half of the sixteenth century was described as decorated with cut work, but it is difficult to say just how soon it had developed to a point that could be called lace. That in Plate 9 is rather to be considered as embroidery, but as more and more linen was cut away, and only small groups of threads were left in either direction to support the needle-made design, the work can truly be described as lace. This is *reticella*, and it leads to the whole exciting range of needlepoint laces. Plate 10, probably a fragment from a late sixteenth century shirt, shows this very well. One could easily suppose that the band of reticella through the middle of the linen was a separate insertion. This is not so. The side pieces of linen have never been cut apart; and the lace was built on very small groups of horizontal threads and two larger groups of vertical threads left of the original fabric. The horizontal threads are only occasionally continuous across the whole band. They mostly terminate on the broader vertical groups. Large covers, of the fashionable chequered type, were frequently built up from separately made sections of reticella and linen (Plate 13). This would be a much easier method than doing all the work in one piece.

In the second half of the sixteenth century

Plate 4   Panels of Lacis, Italian. Late sixteenth century. a. White linen and coloured silks. 112 × 29 cm. b. White linen. Width 24 cm.

reticella was often used as a border for ruffs, collars and cuffs, and for household linen. It was then usually enriched with an additional edging of lace points (Plates 11 to 14). This was slight and narrow at first, but its introduction was a very important step, because it was the first needlepoint lace to be made without a founda-tion of linen or netting. It was called *Punto in Aria*, literally meaning 'stitch in the air'. During the last quarter of the century the collars, and the lace, grew wider and richer, to become one of the most important decorative features of cos-tume from about 1585. They were stiffened with starch, which was first introduced into England from Flanders in about 1564. It could be tinted to make them yellow, pale blue, or perhaps other colours, but this must have been comparatively rare as it is not often seen in contemporary por-traits. The larger collars and ruffs also needed the support of wire frames. This extraordinary fashion lasted until about 1625 or 1630 and is

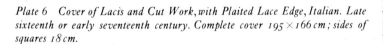

Plate 5 Panel of Lacis, Italianate design, but probably Flemish. Early seventeenth century. Lacis only, 46×43 cm.

Plate 6 Cover of Lacis and Cut Work, with Plaited Lace Edge, Italian. Late sixteenth or early seventeenth century. Complete cover 195×166 cm; sides of squares 18 cm.

Plate 7   Border of Altar Frontal, Twisted netting with Darned-in Pattern, 'Buratto'. The netting is a golden yellow. Late sixteenth or early seventeenth century. Width 13.5 cm.

occasionally shown in even later portraits.

The process of making Punto in Aria is interesting because it continued to be used, with minor adaptations, for all subsequent needle-made laces. The design was drawn on parchment, and one or more linen threads were couched over the framing lines and the outlines of the pattern. These couching stitches passed through the parchment to hold the outlines in position while the lace was being made, but after this stage, all the rest of the work was on the surface. The supporting threads of the design were buttonholed or overcast, and the solid areas filled with rows of buttonhole stitches worked over the outline thread, and then into each other, row by row. These could be made so closely as to give an absolutely solid surface, or be spaced out regularly to give open contrasting

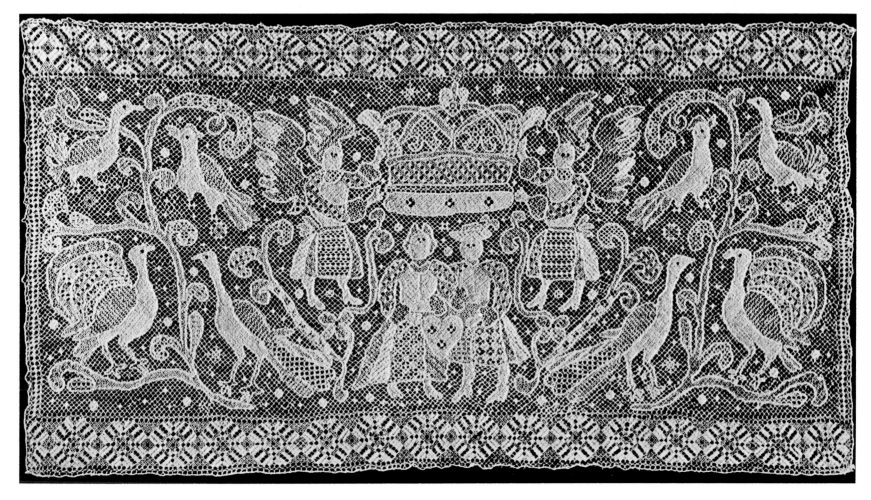

Plate 8 Panel of Lacis, German. Seventeenth century. 65 × 34 cm.

effects (Plate 14*c*). The solid areas, known as the *toilé*, were connected by such bars as would be necessary to hold the design in place after it had been freed from the parchment. These are called either 'bars' or 'brides'. They too were worked over and decorated with picots and loops. When the work was complete the stitches at the back of the parchment were cut to release the lace, and the parchment could be used again.

Plate 11 shows a normal geometric reticella border, with alternating patterns, of a type that was made in many countries during the later part of the sixteenth century. It has been cut from the plain linen on which it was made, but the narrow lower edge, to which the matching Punto in Aria was sewn, shows that it was fairly heavy, of the sort used for table-cloths and bed

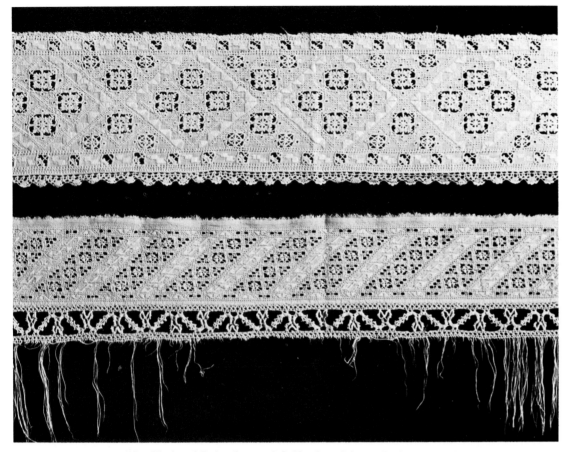

Plate 9   Two Borders of Cut Work and Embroidery, with Bobbin Lace Edgings. Early seventeenth century.
Widths 13 cm and 10.5 cm.

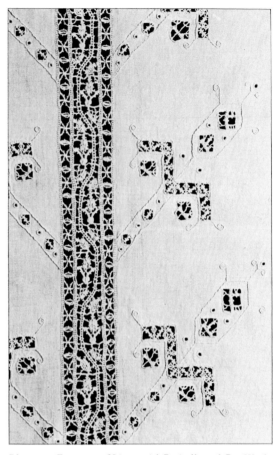

Plate 10   Fragment of Linen, with Reticella and Cut Work.
Late sixteenth century. 44 × 35 cm.

linen, or in the church for altar cloths and frontals. The very fine corner of a border in Plate 12 was almost certainly made in Venice, and has been cut from a handkerchief. The narrow edge of linen here is fine smooth lawn, and it would be most unusual to find a piece of this period more delicate than this. In both cases the threads used for the lace-making are a little

coarser than those of the weaving but are closely related to them. The designs of fine lace were naturally more elaborate than those of coarser pieces.

Geometric patterns were the easiest to construct in the square and rectangular spaces of cut linen, and the earliest examples of reticella and Punto in Aria were all of this kind. They

continued to be used for furnishing for a very long time. The two samplers of cut work, drawn thread and geometric reticella in Plate 24 are not dated, but are probably as late as the second half of the seventeenth century. Fashion changed more swiftly for lace intended to be worn on costume. Even here, geometric designs were still frequently used throughout the first quarter of the seventeenth century, although before 1600 more ambitious and very beautiful designs with formalized flowers, people, birds and animals were being worked by skilful lace-workers.

Pattern books of lace designs were printed in Italy, France, England and other countries in the sixteenth and seventeenth centuries. A particularly successful one by Federico Vinciolo, a Venetian, was published in Paris in 1587 and reprinted in numerous editions in different countries. It was dedicated to the Queen of France and entitled *Les Singuliers et Nouveaux Pourtraicts et Ouvrages de Lingerie*. Another famous pattern book printed many times, the *Corona delle Nobile et Virtuose Donne* by Cesare Vecellio, was first published in Venice in 1592. Ordinary people travelled very little in the past, but these and many other similar books, and the very lively international lace trade, kept lace-makers and their patrons well aware of fashionable trends. They also helped to encourage the increasing technical skill of the lace-workers of the period, for many of the designs they contained were very elaborate, using graceful curves without the limitations of a rectangular framework. Plate 16 shows such a design carried out most beautifully. In this lace both the straight part of the border and the pointed edge are Punto in Aria, worked over a parchment design. It is an exceptional piece, and has a little work in relief to emphasize details. The reticella border in Plate 15 is also unusual and interesting, with its figures, birds and trees. This too has some relief decoration. The lines on the costumes of the lady and gentleman are represented by covered threads attached only at the ends, so that they can move slightly.

The large cover shown in Plate 17 is Italian cut work and Punto in Aria, of the late sixteenth

Plate 11   Reticella with Punto in Aria edging. Late sixteenth century. Together 20 cm wide.

Plate 12   Reticella and Punto in Aria Border from a Handkerchief, Venetian. Early seventeenth century. Width 14 cm.

or very early seventeenth century. It is far richer in design than the simple cut work in the earlier plates. The broad strapwork of linen that frames the figure panels was cut in an ogee pattern similar to the basic designs of many important woven silks and velvets of the period. Details of the cover in Plates 18 and 19 show some of the Punto in Aria panels of classical gods and goddesses in their chariots. They were worked entirely in buttonhole stitch, with tiny black glass beads for eyes. The early seventeenth century vertical border, Plate 20, is also cut work, but the design looks very much as if it were intended for Punto in Aria. In this piece the whole pattern has been cut from a single strip of linen, and only the bars, the open fillings and the cut edges are worked in buttonhole stitch. Elaborate though it is, this is much quicker work than Punto in Aria. It is interesting to compare it with the border shown in Plate 21, which really is Punto in Aria.

The sharply pointed edging lace that was so perfectly suited to stiffened and wired collars and ruffs gradually changed towards a slightly more rounded form during the early seventeenth century, although the standing collars remained in fashion for the first twenty-five or thirty years in most countries. In the second quarter of the century there was a far greater change. Heavy padding and stiffening of clothes went out of fashion, linen was more lightly starched, and the wire supports for collars were discarded, so that they fell down naturally on to the shoulders. Their lace borders no longer retained anything of the pointed effect, but instead had fully rounded scallops; at first these were rich and deep, but by about 1635 or 1640, and particularly in the Netherlands, they became broad and quite shallow. This scalloped

Plate 13   *Cover of reticella, Punto in Aria and Cut Work. Late sixteenth or early seventeenth century. Whole cover 172 × 138 cm; this piece 61 × 48 cm.*

12

lace is known as Collar Lace (Plates 23 and 35a). The whole style of dress had changed from the rigidly formal and artificial shapes that disguised the figure to a much more natural and graceful recognition of it.

All this applied equally to the dress of men and women, and there was no difference at all in the sort of lace worn by either. The fineness, width and elaboration was a matter of cost and personal taste alone. In Elizabethan England a richly decorated shirt could be very expensive. In 1583 Philip Stubbs wrote in his *Anatomie of Abuses*, 'I have heard of shirtes that have cost some ten shillynges, some twenty, some forty, some five pounds, some twenty nobles, and which is horrible to heare some ten pounds a pece.' This puritanical gentleman inveighing against luxury may have exaggerated a little. Even so, multiplying his figures by forty or fifty to give their equivalent value today, his crescendo is quite impressive. In 1640 Charles I paid £25 and £35 for single shirt collars; and one French courtier, in the early seventeenth century, boasted that he had thirty-two acres of the best vineyard property around his neck.

Bobbin Lace

The earliest pattern books containing designs for bobbin lace were printed in the second half of the sixteenth century, but it is probable that narrow edgings and simple insertions to decorate seams were being made early in the century. The Italians and Flemish both claim to have been the inventors of bobbin lace, but as the development from a fancy woven braid to a slightly open insertion would have been a very natural and easy one, it might have come about independently in more than one place.

Plate 14a   Punto Avorio, a variety of Punto in Aria, closely worked with needle-made knots, and supposed to look like ivory. Late sixteenth century. Width 9.5 cm.

Plate 14b.   Fine Reticella and Punto in Aria, Italian. Late sixteenth century. Width 9.5 cm.

Plate 14c   Punto in Aria. Late sixteenth or early seventeenth century. Width 11.5 cm.

Plate 15   Reticella Border, with Figures and Birds, Italian. End of sixteenth or early seventeenth century. Width 13 cm.

Plate 16   Punto in Aria, Italian. Early seventeenth century. Width 16.5 cm.

The design for bobbin lace was drawn on parchment and pricked to fix the position of pins that were to control the pattern. This was stretched over a pillow firmly stuffed with straw, and pins were stuck through the prearranged holes into the pillow, leaving about half their length standing free. The lace-maker twisted and plaited the threads between these pins to form the lace; it was a sort of weaving process. Each thread was carried on a separate lace-bobbin, which was convenient for the worker to hold and manipulate and which, by its weight, held the thread under a light tension. The slender bobbins, usually about nine or ten centimetres long, were made of wood, bone, or occasionally of metal, and the thread was wound round a narrow neck near the top. Forty or fifty bobbins might be used to make a narrow simple lace, but many hundred would be needed for a fine wide border. In sixteenth century England bobbin lace was sometimes called 'bone lace', and it is possible that actual small bones were used as bobbins.

The brides or the mesh ground of bobbin lace are formed of either plaited or twisted threads, and the solid areas have a texture very much like that of plain woven linen or muslin. This is appropriately called the 'clothwork' or the *toilé*, a word derived from the French *toile*, meaning linen cloth, and also used for the solid part of needlepoint lace. The differences between the textures of bobbin lace and needlepoint are shown in the enlarged photographs of Plates 129 to 132. They are usually easily distinguishable, but if the lace in question is extremely fine a magnifying glass may be helpful. Often the mere feeling of the lace is enough, bobbin work being more pliable than needlepoint. This is particularly noticeable with Flemish work. Their lace

Plate 17   Cover of Cut Linen, with Figure Panels of Punto in Aria, Italian. Late sixteenth or early seventeenth century. 147×144cm.

Plate 18   Detail from Plate 17, showing the Central Panel with Apollo in his Sun Chariot. Punto in Aria Panel, 24×21 cm.

Plate 19   Detail from Plate 17, with Venus and Cupid in a Chariot drawn by Doves, and showing the Plaited Lace Edging. Punto in Aria Panel, 26×21 cm.

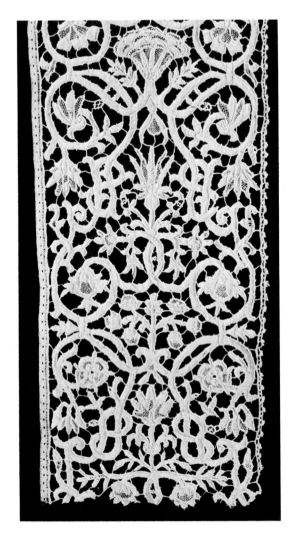

Plate 21 Punto in Aria Border, probably Italian. Second quarter of the seventeenth century. Width 17 cm.

Plate 20 Vertical Border of Cut Linen, with Needlepoint Fillings. Early seventeenth century. 36 × 16.5 cm.

was softer than the Italian as it was usually more openly worked. In the eighteenth century the best Flemish thread was incredibly fine. Probably nobody else ever quite equalled it.

Plate 25a shows an early braid-like insertion used to decorate a seam, with a narrow drawn

thread edge to the linen on both sides. It is impossible to give an exact date to a simple fragment like this – it may be seventeenth century country work – but it is from this sort of work that bobbin lace was developing in the middle of the sixteenth century. Later in the

century the lace could be more open and elaborate, its designs usually based on those of geometric reticella and Punto in Aria, which were the more fashionable laces. These bobbin laces imitated the rectangular framework of supporting bars that in reticella were the essential

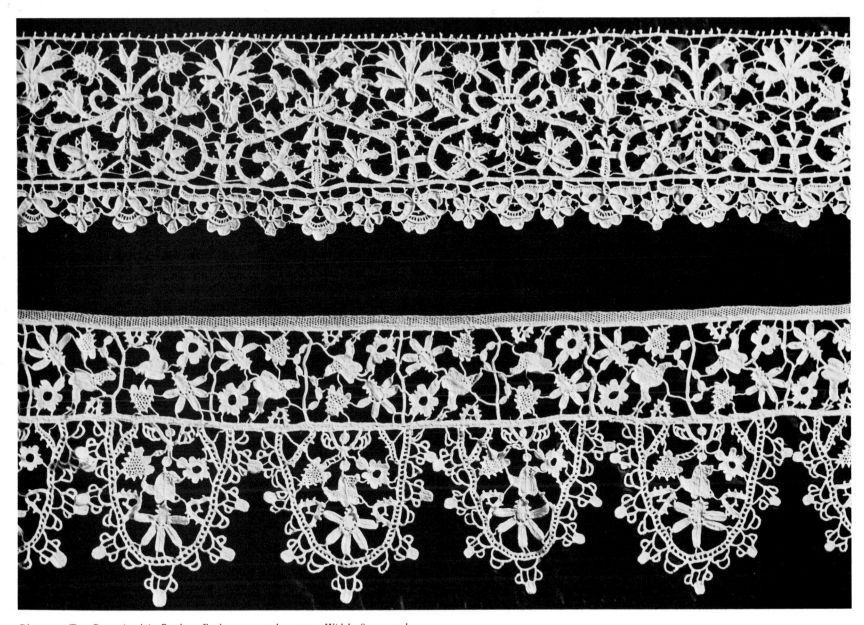

Plate 22   Two Punto in Aria Borders. Early seventeenth century. Widths 8.5 cm and 12.5 cm.

Plate 23a Needlepoint Collar Lace, English or Flemish, c. 1630. Width 8 cm.

Plate 23b Needlepoint Border, similar in design to Collar Lace but heavier, for use on domestic or church linen. Italian, c. 1630. Width 15.5 cm.

Plate 24 Two English Samplers of Cut Work, Drawn Thread and Reticella, c. 1650–80. 34 × 13.5 cm and 46 × 17 cm.

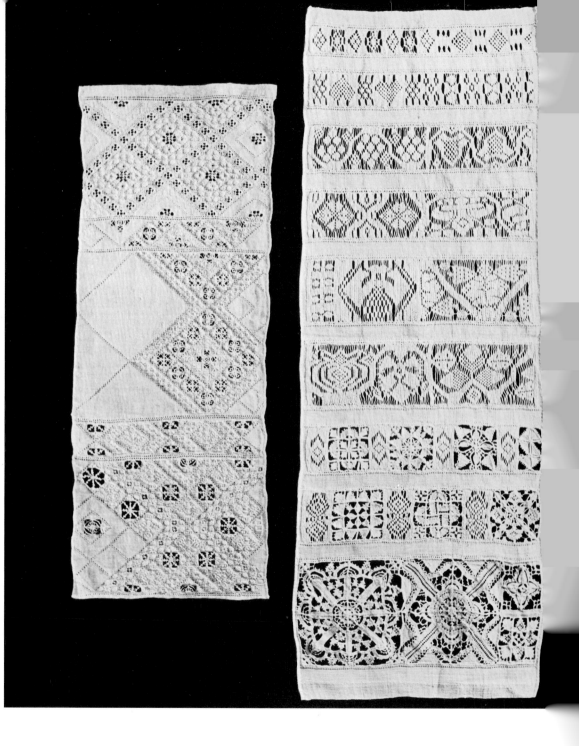

remaining threads of the cut linen base. Plates 25 and 27 show some of these designs, and an amusing example on Plate 26*b* has three repeating sections: a lady, a gentleman, and the double-headed eagle of the Holy Roman Empire. The craftsman, anxious to give his figures all their fingers, has made the hands a bit large. Some of these early laces were almost entirely made of interlacing plaited bars, varying a little in width, but with very little clothwork. They are known as 'plaited lace', and are usually rather simple, but firm and strong and quite attractive (Plates 19 and 28*a*).

The designs used for bobbin lace followed just the same changes of fashion as those of needlepoint. They moved from the purely geometric to the freer style with conventionalized flowers and scrolling stems, and also from the pointed borders of the sixteenth century to rounded scallops for collar lace in the second quarter of the seventeenth century. On Plate 29 a Punto in Aria border is shown with a comparable border of bobbin lace. Both are Italian, of the early seventeenth century, and there are several points of similarity in the two designs. The straight bobbin border on Plate 26*c* was less skilfully made, and the scrolls look rather battered, but the style of the design is again similar.

The worker who made the remarkable border shown on Plate 31 was evidently unwilling to concede that bobbin lace had to be simpler, or in any way inferior to needlepoint. This piece is unusually sophisticated in design, very richly worked in relief, and with a great variety of textures. Some of the flowers were constructed of separately made overlapping layers of petals.

The broad laces on Plates 32, 33 and 34 would probably have been used for domestic or church

Plate 25a   Early Narrow Braid-like Bobbin Lace, used to enrich a seam. Width 3.5 cm.

Plates 25b and c   Early Bobbin Laces, copying Reticella Designs. Peasant Lace of much later periods was often made in similar style and weight to 25c. Widths 4.5 cm and 10 cm.

Plate 27   Border of Bobbin Lace copying Reticella and Punto in Aria, Italian. Late sixteenth century. Width 14 cm.

Plate 26a (opposite)   Bobbin Lace in the style of Reticella, Genoese. Late sixteenth century. Width 4.5 cm.

Plate 26b (opposite)   Bobbin Lace, perhaps made for a marriage, Italian. Late sixteenth century. Width 6.5 cm.

Plate 26c (opposite)   Bobbin Lace in the style of Punto in Aria, Italian. Seventeenth century. Width 7 cm.

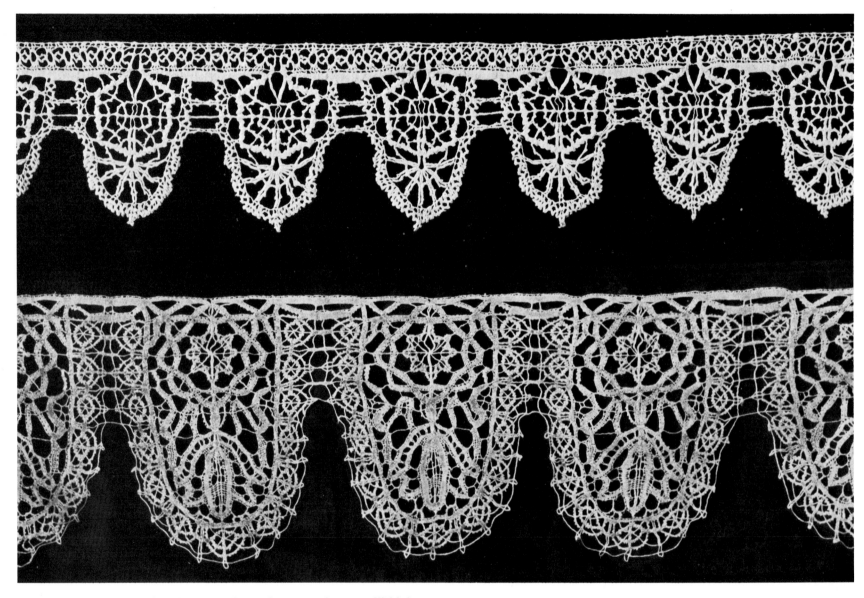

Plate 28a Plaited Lace, Italian. Late sixteenth or early seventeenth century. Width 8.5 cm.

Plate 28b Bobbin-made Collar Lace, Italian or Flemish. Early seventeenth century. Width 13 cm.

Plate 29a   Punto in Aria, Italian. Early seventeenth century. Width 14.5 cm.

Plate 29b   Bobbin Lace, Italian. Early seventeenth century. Width 16 cm.

These two designs have several similar features.

furnishings, or on vestments, but they are very similar in style to the narrower collar lace worn at the same time. Furnishing and church lace did not necessarily follow fashion as closely as dress lace, but there was no such clear distinction between them as that which existed in the nineteenth century. During earlier periods the difference was mainly in the weight of the thread. Finer and therefore more costly lace was worn, and the coarser used for other decoration. Nevertheless, a rich man at this time might well have had finer lace around his table-cloth than his poorer neighbour was wearing.

Plate 32 is of lace made in about 1635 in Genoa. The little seed-like forms are typical of the work from this important centre of bobbin lace-making. In the nineteenth century the same seed or grain shapes were used in Maltese lace, which was based on the early Genoese work. Plate 33 shows a rather later border of about the middle of the seventeenth century, made of a continuous narrow tape formed in position on the lace pillow, following all the curves of the design and varying in width as necessary. Rather obscurely it represents a double-headed bird. This may be Italian, but the same process was used both by the Flemish and the Dutch, and also often in peasant lace, but with much simpler designs. The third of these broad borders, Plate 34, is Flemish, probably made in Antwerp, where symmetrical designs of flowers in vases, like this one, were often produced. They are known as *Potten Kant*, the word *kant* meaning lace. Most of the specimens now left were made in the eighteenth and nineteenth centuries; they have less boldly drawn designs, a different réseau which forms six pointed star-like shapes, and have straight edges. This border must have been made soon after the middle of

Plate 30a   *Punto in Aria, with Bobbin Collar Lace Edging. Early seventeenth century. Width together 13 cm.*

Plate 30b   *Bobbin Edging Lace. Early seventeenth century. Width 7 cm.*

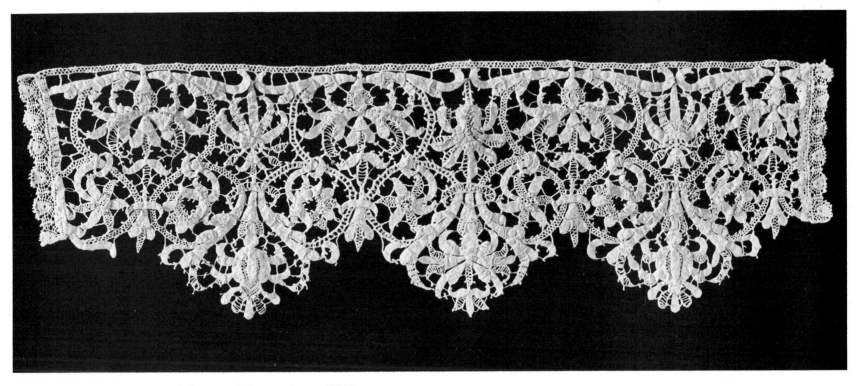

Plate 31   Elaborate Bobbin-made Collar Lace, Italian, c. 1630–40. Width 11.5 cm.

the seventeenth century, perhaps about 1660. The shallow scallops, the bold fullness of the design and the rather uneven early mesh ground all help to determine its date.

Dutch lace of about this period has a very closely woven appearance, with a full design and a thick réseau, which does not give much contrast of tone, so that from a little distance the pattern is quite inconspicuous (Plate 35*b* and *c*). Although not a spectacular lace, it is gently attractive, and to the touch the even surface gives a very pleasant cool linen feeling. Dutch thread at this period was not usually very fine,

so most of their lace was substantial and strong. The deep scallops fashionable for Collar Lace from about 1625 to 1635, or a little later, gradually became shallower (Plate 35*a*). By the middle of the century straight-edged borders were beginning to replace them altogether (Plate 35*c*).

Gold and Silver Lace, and Silk Lace

There are some mouth-watering entries in the *Accounts of the Keepers of the Great Wardrobe* of Queen Elizabeth I's time, and in her *Inventories of New Year's Gifts*, of gold and silver

lace, coloured silk lace, bone lace of silver and black silk, and collars of cut work sewn with spangles and with precious stones and pearls. The metal thread lace itself was bobbin lace, but cut work and reticella were evidently sometimes enriched with added embroidery and edgings of gold. Elizabeth's reign was a period of the most lavish decoration possible; jewels were often sewn over patterned silk and embroidered garments, and courtiers might wear their fortunes on their backs.

Of all this only fragments remain: a little gold lace on gloves, or narrow edgings on an

Plate 32 Bobbin Lace Border, Genoese, c. 1630–35. Width 25.5 cm.

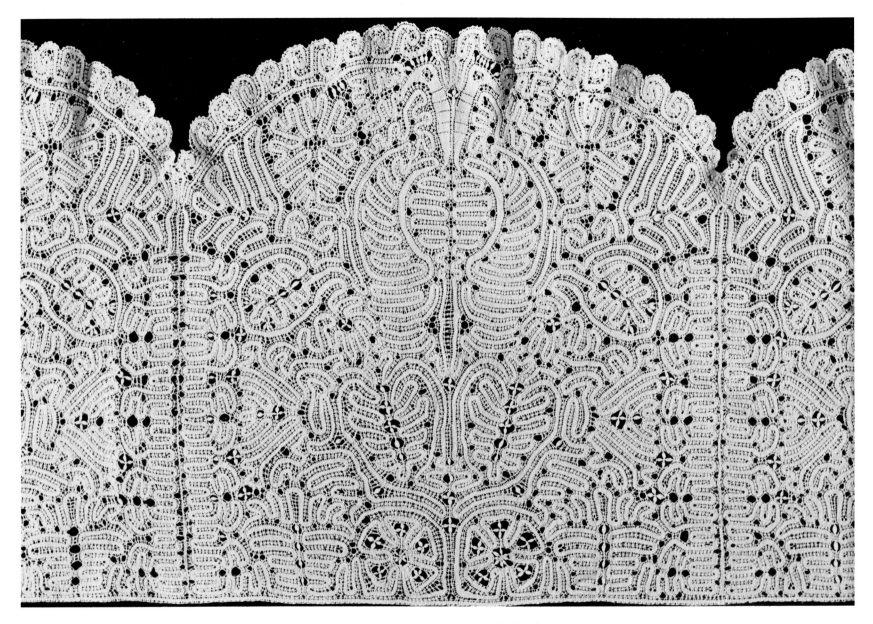

Plate 33   Bobbin Lace Border, probably Italian, c. 1640–50. The design includes a double-headed bird. Width 28 cm.

Plate 34   Bobbin Lace Border, 'Potten Kant', Flemish, probably made in Antwerp, c. 1655–60. Width 25.5 cm.

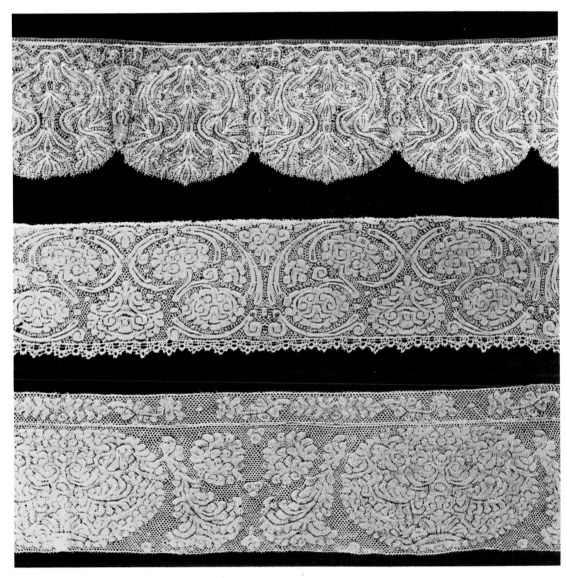

embroidered cap or bodice. The greater the intrinsic value of an object, the less likely it was to survive after its original use was over. Jewels were removed to be used again and again, and gold and silver lace was destroyed to recover the metal. Such pieces as remain are nearly always so light that the metal would not be worth the trouble of recovery.

There is a little silk Punto in Aria and bobbin-made Collar Lace of the early seventeenth century still in existence, made of natural creamy-coloured silk, but now somewhat darkened with age (Plate 36). Both these examples have been treated with a stiffening substance which, unlike starch, will not wash out, so that the lace still stands out rigidly after about 350 years. The designs are like those of the usual linen lace of the same types. Some beautiful coloured silk cloths with Buratto borders have also survived, the netting often in a dyed linen thread, with coloured silk embroidery, sometimes enriched with a little metal thread and gilt sequins. These were made in Italy during the sixteenth and seventeenth centuries.

Plate 35a Bobbin Collar Lace, Flemish, c. 1635–45. Width 8 cm.

Plate 35b Bobbin Lace Border, Dutch, c. 1650–60. Width 7.5 cm.

Plate 35c Bobbin Lace Border, Dutch, c. 1650–60. Width 9.5 cm.

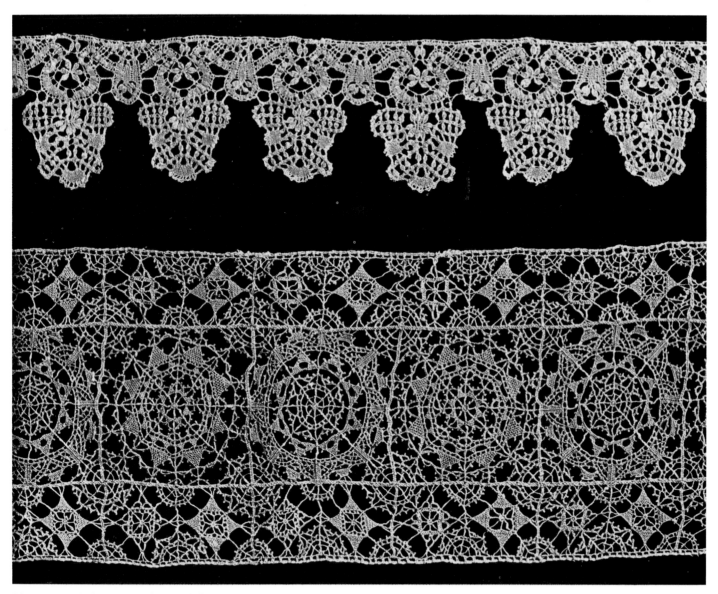

Plate 36 Early Seventeenth Century Silk Lace.
    a. Bobbin Collar Lace, Genoese. Width 6.5 cm.
    b. Punto in Aria, with Reticella style of Design, Italian. Width 13 cm.

III. Mid and Late Seventeenth Century – The Richness of the Baroque

By the middle of the seventeenth century the craft of lace-making was about a hundred years old – only three or four generations of workers. In this little time it had been established and reached maturity, which would hardly have been possible had those hundred years not begun in Renaissance Italy, where all the arts were encouraged by princely patronage, and had it not also been a period of growing wealth and cultured luxury for much of the aristocracy of Europe.

Once Punto in Aria had been achieved, the attraction of lace lay as much in the exciting outlines that it made possible as in the open texture of the fabric. This was fully exploited by the points and scallops of the early lace, but by the middle of the century they were no novelty, and straight-edged lace was beginning to replace even the shallow scallops of the 1640s. The designer had far greater freedom working on a large scale within a continuous border than in one where each point or scallop was a separate unit, with the border behind it designed as a series of similar but rectangular compartments. Beautiful as the early lace certainly is, this rather primitive limitation must have been irksome to some designers. The magnificent scrolling baroque ornament, characteristic of seventeenth century art, could not be confined to such compartments, but it flourished joyfully in the new broad straight-sided lace (Plates 37, 38 and 39).

No artistic movement ever occurs suddenly, without any prelude. Some of the more ambitious designs, especially where the straight part of a lace border was of major importance, had forecast this liberation earlier in the century (Plate 21). Designers in Italy would have been fully aware of the baroque style of ornament before its normal use in lace design, as it had been used there in other crafts and in architectural decoration since the later part of the sixteenth century.

Needlepoint Lace

Venetian Rose Point laces overshadowed all others from about 1650 to late in the seventeenth century; they were the most desired luxury of fashion. The word 'rose' in this context means 'raised'; that is, with work in relief. It does not refer in any way to the flower.

From the earliest days of lace the Venetians had made the finest needlepoint obtainable, but their skill was uniquely demonstrated in this most elaborate lace, in preserving the beautiful drawing of their designers, the strength of form and line, and in the wonderful relief work. These laces have today an almost magical way of conjuring up visions of the richness of the whole period.

The general name Venetian Point can be used to describe the differing, but related, types of lace that were developed from each other during this half-century. They were all designed with scrolling stems, vigorously drawn, fully using all the width of the lace, and with richly ornate conventional flowers. At first the lace was bold and magnificent; gradually, and without any abrupt change in the style of design, the scale of the motifs was reduced and the lace appeared lighter. Near the end of the century the effect had become completely different, with an elaborate texture of tiny forms. These were still reminiscent of the earlier designs but very much reduced in size, and were used to create a very delicate and more feminine style. There were no sharp divisions between these varieties; they merged and overlapped.

The first of these broad types, made between about 1650 and 1665, is known as *Gros Point*, not at all implying that the workmanship was coarse, but only that the scale of the design was large and noble (Plates 37, 38 and 39). The bold relief and the very close buttonholing, of which the solid areas are formed, make it a heavy lace, although the thread is usually fine. Gros Point was a superb lace for church use. Laid nearly flatly, to show its magnificence, it was very effective even when seen from a distance, but it was by no means made exclusively for the Church.

The intermediate style, from about 1660 to 1695, has no name other than Rose Point, which in its general meaning of raised needle-made lace also covers the whole family. This lace, if worn as a lady's collar, as it was in the earlier part of this period, was still spread smoothly

Plate 37   Venetian Gros Point Flounce, c. 1655–65. Width 24 cm.

Plate 38   Venetian Gros Point Border, c. 1655–65. Width 14 cm.

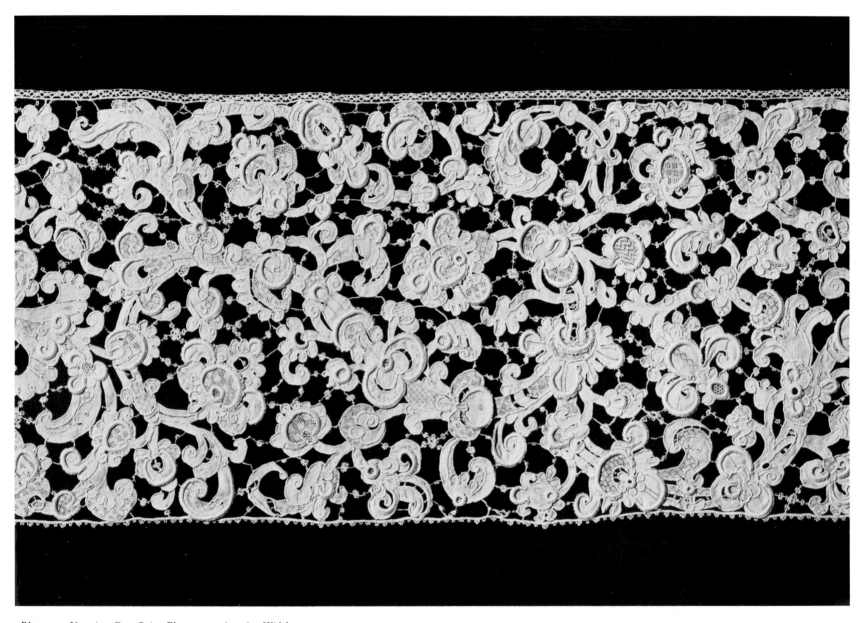

Plate 39   Venetian Gros Point Flounce, c. 1655–65. Width 22.5 cm.

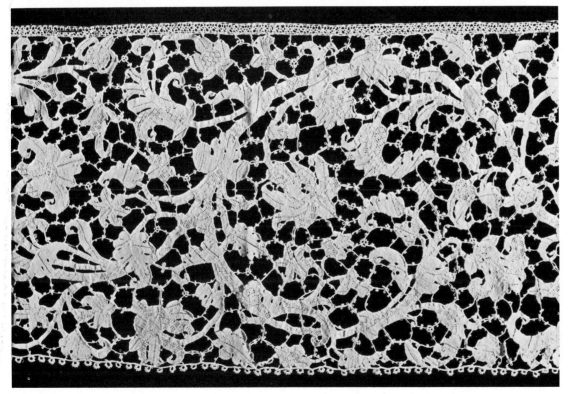

Plate 40a   Part of a Venetian Gros Point Border, with Animals in the Design, c. 1655–65. Width 11.5 cm.

Plate 40b   Venetian Flat Point Border, c. 1660–70. Width 18.5 cm.

around her shoulders. Later, when the collar was not so fashionable, it was used, with a little fullness, as neck and sleeve trimmings of the shift, which showed within the low neckline of the dress and at the elbow. Rose Point was not really soft enough to be gathered but could be eased a little as it was seamed on, or the linen to which it was sewn could be lightly gathered. Men wore it in the same way at the wrist, and the very elaborately dressed could have a sort of flounce, just below the knee, called a 'canon'. Their collars, of the shape known as *col rabat*, were square-fronted, and had deep panels of either Gros Point or Rose Point at each side of the opening, as in Plate 41. They were worn close under the chin, and the heavy wigs of the time covered most of the back where the lace was narrower. Between about 1665 and 1670 the col rabat was gradually replaced by the cravat, a long strip of linen with lace ends, that was twisted round the neck and tied at the front, often with a separate bow of ribbon (Plate 44).

The latest of the Venetian Rose Point laces, made from about 1685 until the early years of the next century, has been given the romantic name *Point de Neige*, the amazing intricacy of the relief work and the tiny detail suggesting the lightness of snow-flakes (Plate 45). The design and relief work were sometimes so elaborate and close that the bars holding the lace together were hardly visible. Plates 46 and 47 show a very beautiful piece of Point de Neige made for the type of head-dress known as the *fontange*, and one of the matching pair of lappets. The lace with a curved top would have been pleated into a slightly fan-shaped upright form and supported by a wire frame to stand up above the forehead, with the lappets hanging down from a tiny cap behind it. The fontange was called

Plate 41   Lace from a Gentleman's Collar, Venetian Rose Point, c. 1670. Depth at front 23 cm.

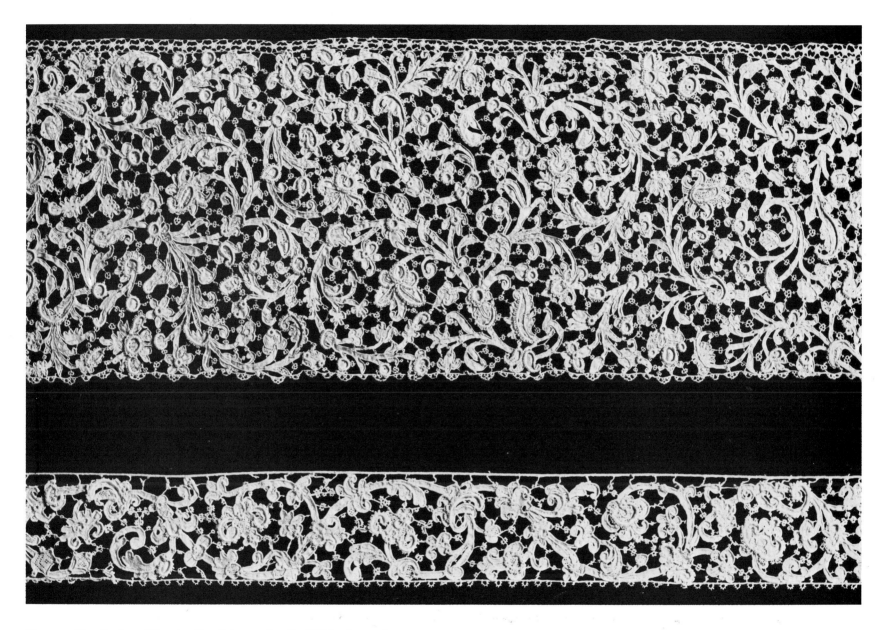

Plate 42   Two Borders of Venetian Rose Point, c. 1675–80. Widths 16 cm and 5 cm.

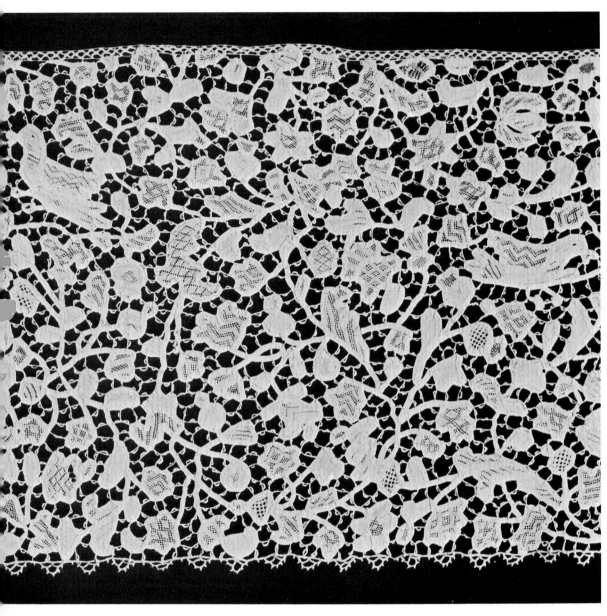

Plate 43 Mezzo Punto or Tape Lace, English. Bobbin-made braid, with needlepoint fillings, c. 1680. Width 23 cm.

after Mlle de Fontanges, one of Louis XIV's mistresses. It is said that her hair became disarranged whilst she was out hunting with the king, and in tying it up with a lace-trimmed kerchief, she produced such a charming coiffure that he asked her to wear it at court in the evening. It was, of course, copied by all the other ladies next day, but alas, developed into a very stiff and formal style that Louis is known to have disliked.

The process of making Venetian Point was basically the same as that described in Chapter II, for Punto in Aria; but apart from the straight edges of the lace there were no framing and supporting geometric shapes. The Rose Point designs filled the lace completely from edge to edge, and were supported only by brides joining the solid parts to each other and to the edges. As the style developed the brides became more numerous and were more richly ornamented. Elaborate relief work replaced the slight touches that had sometimes been used on Punto in Aria. This raised work was the last stage in the making of Rose Point. It was formed by attaching extra linen threads, following the contours of the design, and graduated by adding more and more threads to give greater depth and width to the central part of the raised edge, and then tapering it down again. When the correct shape had been made it was tightly buttonholed over, across the padding threads, and further decorated with loops and picots. The subtlety of the graduation is a clear indication of the quality of Rose Point; to achieve its perfection needed the greatest skill and patience. The narrow *cordonnet* around all the unemphasized edges was buttonholed over a few continuous threads.

The rich effect of Rose Point has often been compared with that of carved ivory, and Grin-

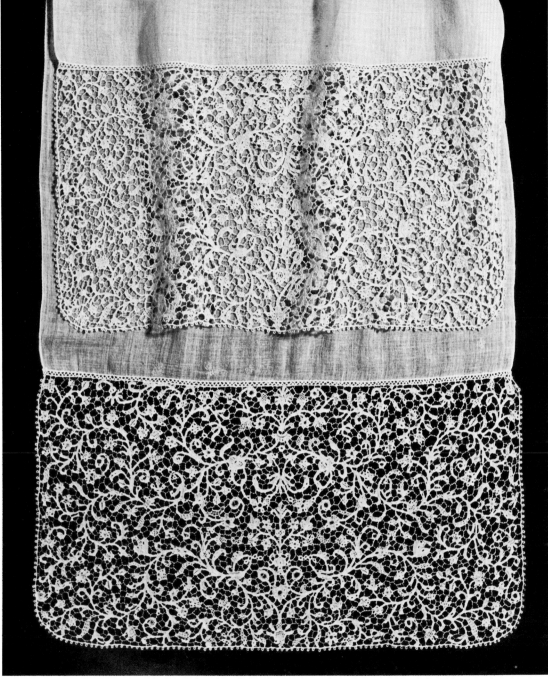

Plate 44   Linen Cravat with Venetian Flat Point Ends, c. 1690–95. Lace ends 35 × 19 cm; Length of Cravat 182 cm.

ling Gibbons, who produced such superb decorative carvings for Charles II and the other late Stuart sovereigns, must have had a similar idea when he saw it worn at court. He was fascinated, and several times included very close copies of the lace in his carved wood panels. This was an age when the *trompe d'œil* in art was much enjoyed. One small carving of the front of a cravat trimmed with Rose Point was actually worn by Horace Walpole at a reception in the eighteenth century. It would have been eighty or a hundred years old at that time, so was hardly fashionable. This delightful little *tour de force* is now in the Victoria and Albert Museum.

Lace made by exactly the same process as Rose Point, but left without the final glory of the relief work, is called *Point Plat* or 'Flat Point' (Plate 40*b*). It was made throughout the same period, and passed through the same changes of fashion from bold to delicate designs. Obviously it was a less costly lace, but admirable when used where its lightness was an advantage (Plate 44).

At the very end of the seventeenth and in the early years of the eighteenth century a debased sort of point lace was made, either flat or with a minimum of raised work, and with an insignificant design that amounted to little more than an all-over texture (Plate 49*a*). It is called *Coralline Point* or 'Mermaids' Lace', as it was supposed to have been based on the branching forms of coral. It represents the last stage in the long and gradual reduction in the scale of the design of Venetian Point lace. Nothing further could develop in this direction, and a new start was inevitable.

Plate 50 shows an interesting survival of the Rose Point style into the eighteenth century. It

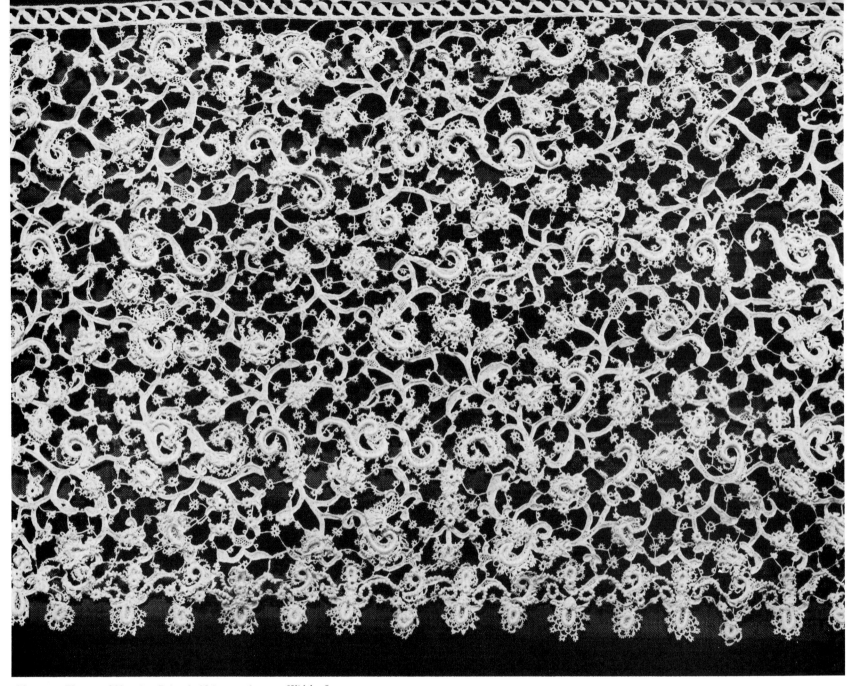

Plate 45   Flounce of Venetian Point de Neige, c. 1690–95. Width 18 cm.

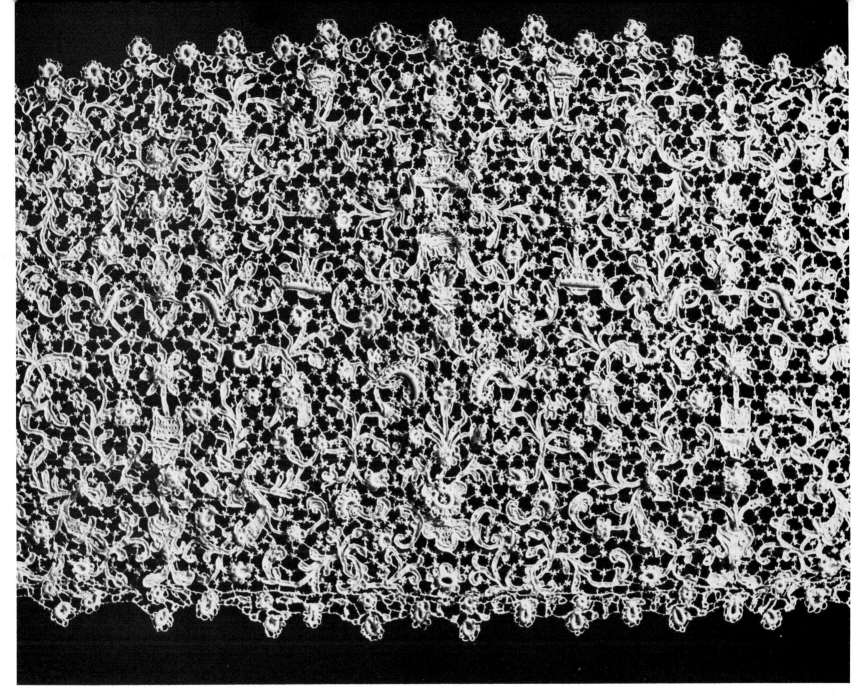

Plate 46   Fontange of Venetian Point de Neige, c. 1695. Greatest depth 18.5 cm; complete length 68 cm.

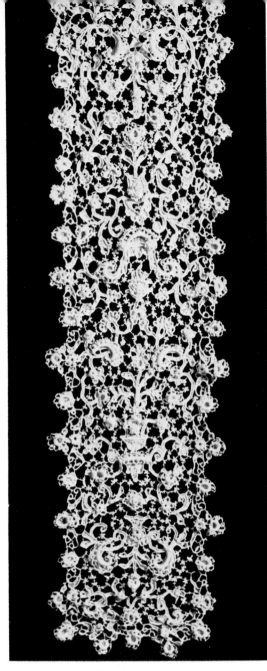

Plate 47 Lappet of Venetian Point de Neige, from the same head-dress as the Fontange in Plate 46, c. 1695. Width 9 cm to 7 cm; complete length 56 cm.

is silk lace, made in Venice, especially for use on the Jewish *tallith*, a scarf worn during public prayers. The earlier examples of this have a ground of brides, like other Rose Point, but this late one has a mesh réseau of eighteenth century type, although it has kept the old Rose Point style of design which was no longer fashionable.

Copies of Venetian Point were made in many countries all through the second half of the seventeenth century, but seldom reached the quality of design or skill of Venetian work. Plate 49*b* shows a Spanish version. The top edge has been cut and some of the design lost, but the endless wriggly line of raised work is typical and somewhat monotonous. It relied on complicated texture rather than beauty of form. This piece may have been made near the end of the seventeenth century; the Spaniards at this time were not following fashion very closely.

The lace in Plate 43 was probably made in England by an amateur worker, round about 1680. This type of lace, known as *Mezzo Punto* or 'Tape Lace', was made by using a bobbin-made braid for the outlines of the pattern, but with needlepoint fillings and brides. In Mezzo Punto the braid was not formed over the design on the lace pillow, as it was for the border in Plate 33, but was just a straight braid made beforehand, and folded or puckered as it was sewn round the outlines of the pattern in preparation for the needlepoint work. Although very unsophisticated, the design of this piece attempted to follow the scrolling forms of the period, but with the addition of little birds and animals among the foliage; two birds appear in the section illustrated. English seventeenth century lace often included rather quaintly drawn creatures scattered about in a lively free-and-easy way. The central panels of the most elaborate lace samplers were even more adventurous, with figure subjects worked in relief like those of English stump work embroidery of the same time.

All the fine laces used so lavishly by seventeenth century aristocrats were expensive, and Venetian Rose Point the most costly of all; as just one example, James II of England paid £36.10s.0d. for a Venetian Point cravat to wear at his coronation in 1685 – this would be the equivalent of well over £1000 today. Very naturally, rulers of the countries importing such luxuries tried desperately to stem the enormous flow of money that they were losing, although they by no means always limited their own personal extravagance. Laws prohibiting the importation of foreign lace were passed one after the other both in France and England.

In 1660 Louis XIV forbade the wearing of all foreign lace, and restricted even the use of French lace. So little did the law succeed that it was followed by others in 1661, 1662 and 1664 reiterating the prohibitions, particularly against Venice and Genoa, where fine bobbin lace and gold and silver lace were made. The King's minister Colbert devised a more ingenious plan. He established thirty Venetian women lacemakers at his château near Alençon, in Normandy, to make lace in the Venetian style and teach the craft to French women. Madame Gilbert, who had been put in charge of the work, brought specimens of the lace to Versailles, where it was exhibited to Louis and his courtiers. He was delighted and granted the name *Point de France* to the lace, and desired that no other sort should be worn at court. In 1665 a company was formed to produce the lace under royal protection, with a grant, and an exclusive privilege for ten years. The venture was

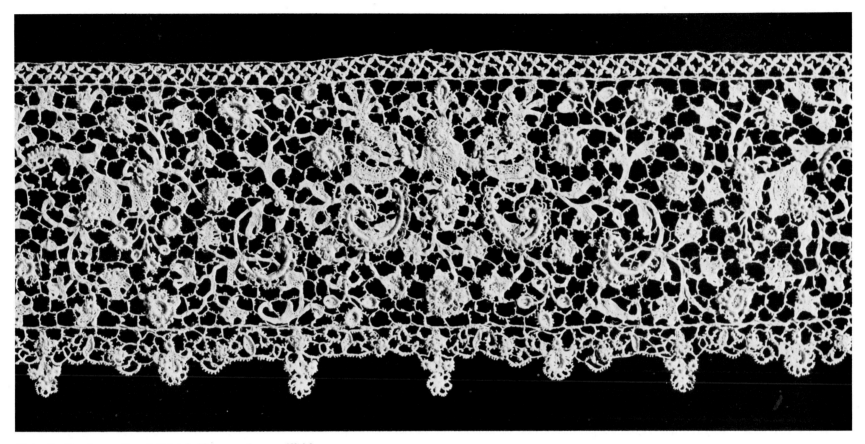

Plate 48 Venetian or French Point de Neige, c. 1690–95. Width 9 cm.

a wonderful success, and French lace production was established on a far higher standard than before, when the lace had been mostly used by the middle classes. Other workers were brought in later and settled at Sedan, Paris and other towns. These included some Flemish bobbin lace-makers, to improve also that side of the craft. France gradually became a great exporting country, earning very large sums

from lace instead of spending heavily on it.

At first the lace made at Alençon was very similar to that from Venice and cannot now be distinguished from it, but French ideas of design soon began to change the style. Under the influence of the great designer Bérain, one of the finest and most original designers of the period, slight and playful architectural forms, and little canopies with looped draperies were introduced

as alternating features. Small scrolling branches, still in the Venetian style, grew from them to fill the intermediate spaces with light decoration. Sometimes tiny figures of musicians and dancers performed under the canopies, and the sunflower, emblem of the Sun King, was included among the flowers. Plate 51 shows a detail from a fine flounce of Point de France with Louis XIV himself, in Roman military costume,

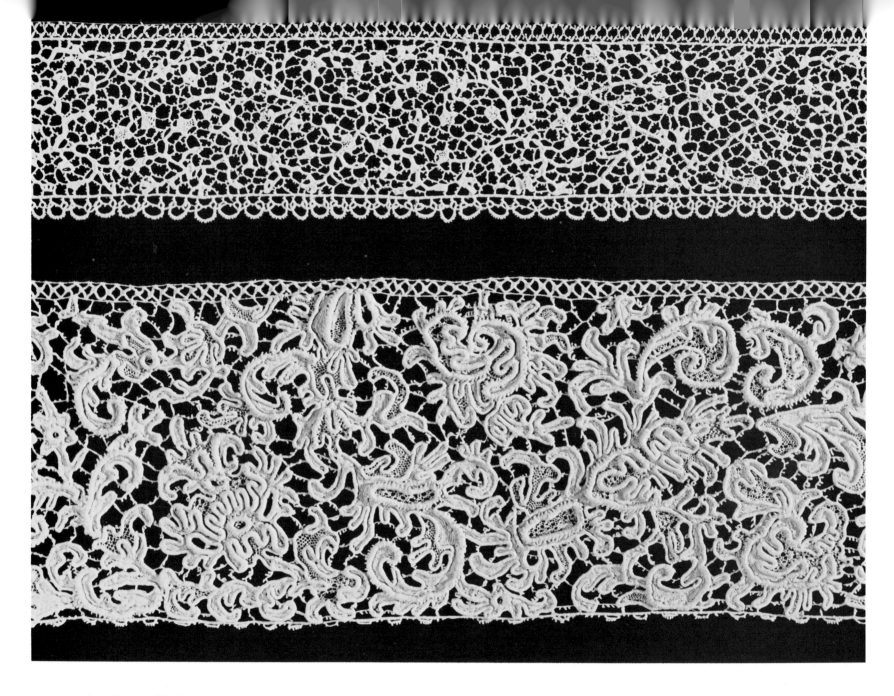

Plate 49a   Late Venetian Flat Point, known as Coralline Point, c. 1695–1705. Width 6.5 cm.   *Plate 49b Spanish Rose Point, c. 1680–90. Width 11.5 cm.*

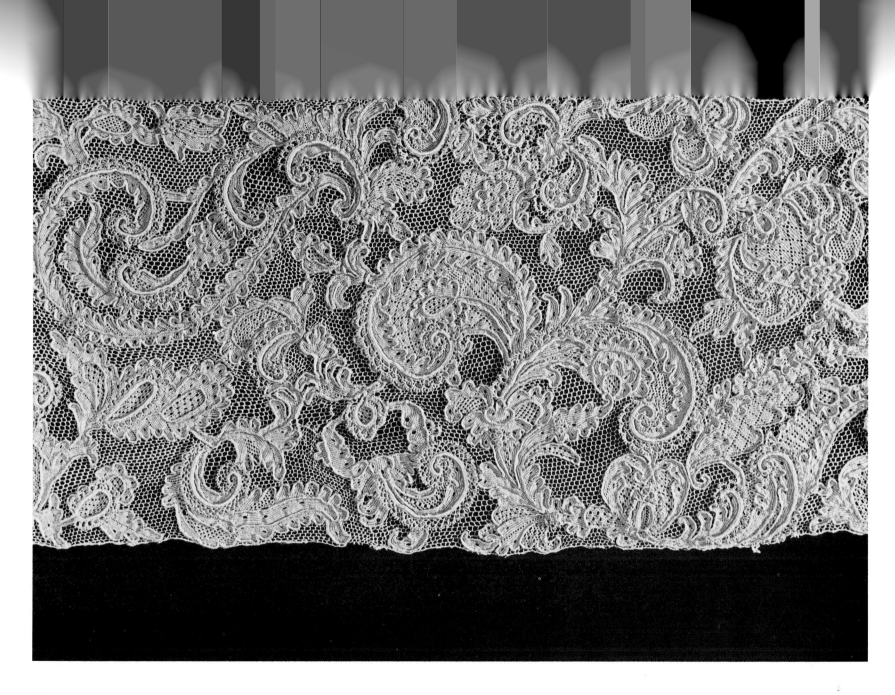

Plate 50   Venétian Silk Rose Point with Réseau, made for use on the Jewish Tallith. Early eighteenth century. Width 14 cm.

standing under a canopy, while two winged figures hold a laurel wreath over his head. Somewhat incongruously for the costume, he is wearing his usual fashionable seventeenth century flowing wig, and is carrying his sceptre with the fleur-de-lis instead of a Roman baton. Above the canopy, but not included in this photograph, the rayed sun is shown, and in another part of the flounce the fleur-de-lis and the royal crown of France are important features. Towards the end of the century the raised work was reduced both in quantity and depth, and some Point de France was quite flat.

On Plate 52 a Point de France lappet is shown with one of Flemish bobbin lace. The influence of the new light-hearted French design can clearly be seen, although the Flemish lappet still has rather larger and heavier motifs, with smaller areas of ground between them. The French lappet, with its asymmetrical and free design, gives a particularly early foretaste of the rococo style which was not to be fully developed until well into the eighteenth century. Another Flemish bobbin lappet on Plate 81a is quite a close copy of the usual more nearly symmetrical style of Point de France design.

The great needlepoint flounce in Plate 54 was probably made at Sedan, where large-scale late baroque designs were often produced. Sedan being near the Flemish frontier and little more than eighty miles from Brussels, it is not surprising that its lace should be rather different in character from the Point de France of Alençon

Plate 51   Detail from a royal Flounce of Point de France, showing Louis XIV as a victorious Roman emperor, c. 1680. Detail 28×20 cm; width of Flounce 62 cm.

and should be influenced by the heavier designs of Flemish work. This flounce could have been one of those so extravagantly used to surround dressing tables, or even baths.

The *toilé* of mid-seventeenth century Venetian Point was joined together by comparatively few brides used only where they were necessary to keep the lace in shape. Gradually they were increased in number to make a more even texture as a background for the design. French lace continued this development, and the ground finally became an almost regular hexagonal pattern of small brides, decorated with picots (Plate 53).

The great advantage France gained from Colbert's efforts was a disaster for Venice. Not only did she lose the vastly profitable French trade, but also by the end of the seventeenth century her leadership in needlepoint lace. The French style of design swept into fashion and Venice had to accept its influence. This can be seen in some examples of Point de Neige, and became dominant in the early eighteenth century grounded Venetian Point (Plates 66*b* and 67), which was the last of the fine laces of Venice before a sad decline.

Bobbin Lace

The midseventeenth century designs for bobbin lace, nearly all for straight-edged borders and flounces, were based on the same rich and formal scrolls as the contemporary needlepoint.

Plate 52a Lappet of Point de France, c. 1690–95. Width 10.5 cm to 7.5 cm; complete length 63 cm.

Plate 52b Lappet of Flemish Bobbin Lace, c. 1695–1700. Width 9 cm to 6.5 cm; complete length 55 cm.

49

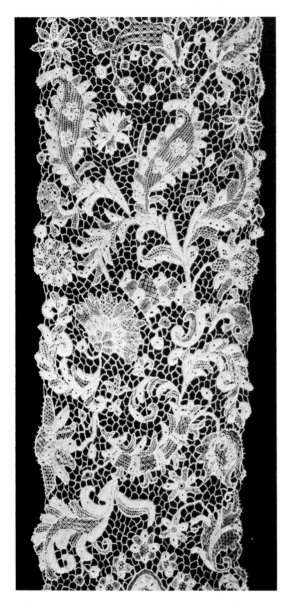

Plate 53 Detail of Point de France Lappet, Plate 52a, c. 1690–95.

Plate 54 French needlepoint Flounce, probably made at Sedan, c. 1700–10. Width 64 cm.

In north Italy, Milan and Genoa were leading centres. Flanders, which traditionally concentrated more on bobbin lace than on needlepoint, became increasingly important as an exporting country. The designs used there were mostly Italianate in character until near the end of the century, when French styles so successfully took the leadership. The Flemish workers adopted the newer fashion and rose to their finest achievements in the early eighteenth century. By the end of the seventeenth century the Italian bobbin lace trade had been severely damaged, both by the increasing skill and popularity of Flemish work, and by the establishment of a higher class of bobbin lace-making in France that followed the success of the Point de France venture.

The noble flounce, Plate 57, is a typical

Plate 55a   *Bobbin Lace Border, North Italian, c. 1650–65. Width 9 cm.*   *Plate 55b*   *Bobbin Lace Border, Italian or Flemish, c. 1655–65. Width 11 cm.*

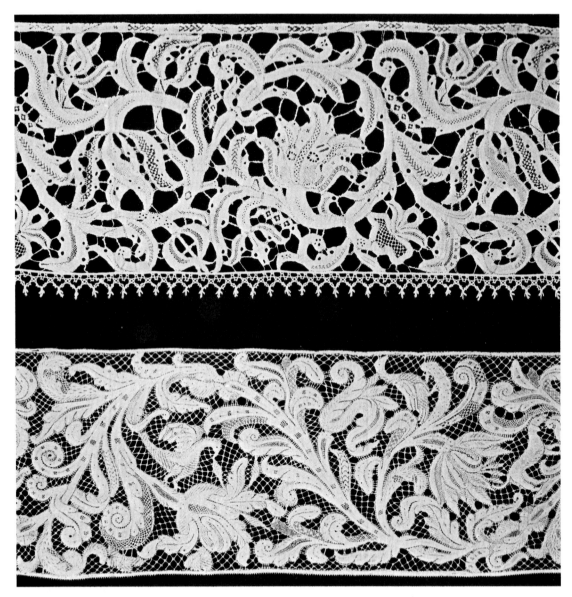

example of Milanese work of about 1660, with symmetrical scrolls growing from a central motif and meeting those of the next repeat to form a well-arranged secondary feature. Plate 58 shows a similarly planned lace, designed as if it were a double border, but made as one piece. It is far less well drawn, but is interesting in having a raised cordonnet and raised dots both on the toilé and occasionally in the fillings. An alternative arrangement of the scrolls was in a continuous flowing movement in one direction, as in Plates 55 and 56. Both forms were used in Venetian Point laces of the same period. One of the flounces with birds and animals in the scrolls, Plate 56b, may be Flemish, as it is more open in texture than most Italian work; the other, Plate 59, gay but irregular, is probably English.

The design in all these borders was made of a more or less continuous braid, which was often enriched with little patterns in the more interesting laces, and could be varied considerably in width, extra bobbins being added as the work proceeded. The groundwork of brides, or mesh, was added separately by hooking the threads of which it was formed into the edges of the clothwork of the design, and at times carrying them in little plaits behind the design to continue the ground in the next space.

The development of the grounds is interesting. At first it was similar to that of Venetian Point. The earliest type, Plate 55, hardly needed any connecting bars at all, as the pattern was proportionately large and the forms touched the edges and each other so frequently. With more elaborate designs brides were essential. At first they were placed irregularly only where they were needed (Plate 56a), and later more closely and evenly (Plate 57), just as in needlepoint.

Plate 56a   Bobbin Lace Flounce, North Italian, c. 1655–65. Width 25 cm.

Plate 56b   Border of Bobbin Lace with Réseau, probably Flemish, c. 1660–65. Width 21 cm.

Plate 57   Bobbin Lace Flounce, Milanese, c. 1655–65. Width 27 cm.

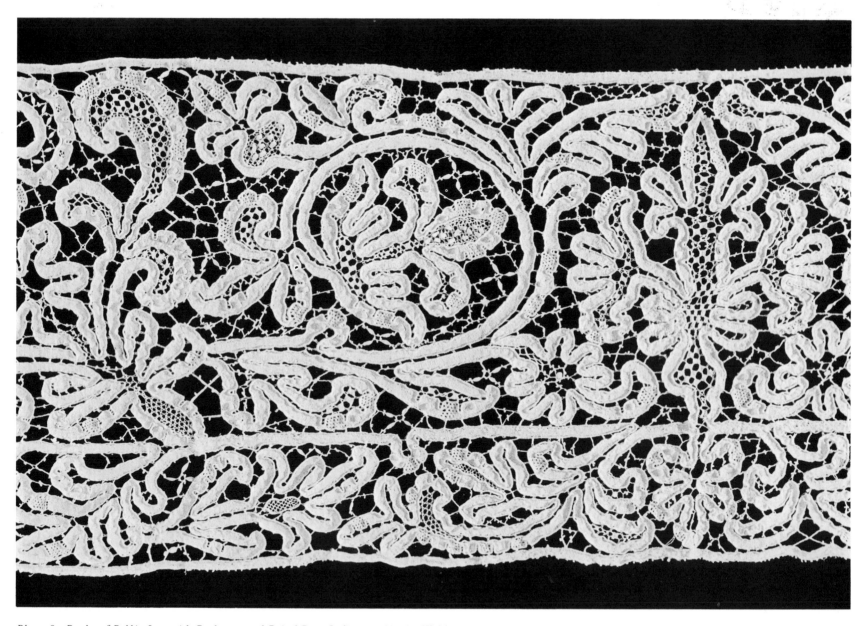

Plate 58   Border of Bobbin Lace with Cordonnets and Raised Dots, Italian, c. 1660–65. Width 21 cm.

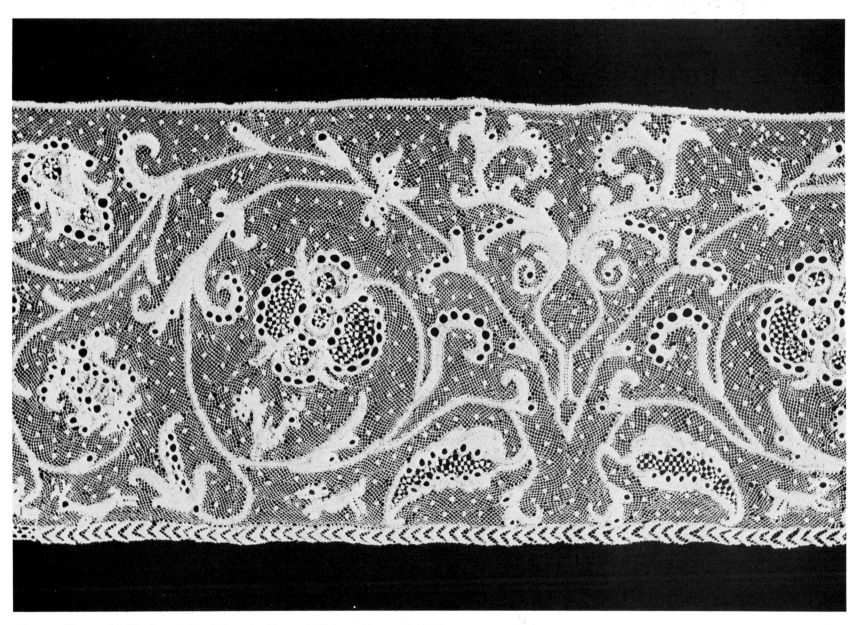

Plate 59   Flounce of Bobbin Lace with early irregular Réseau, English, c. 1665–70. Width 26 cm.

Plate 60   Flounce of Flemish Bobbin Lace with irregular Réseau, c. 1665–80. Width 28 cm.

This style continued for a long time, but from about 1660 some bobbin lace-makers began to use a mesh réseau instead of brides. This was much earlier than in needlepoint lace, where the mesh was not used until the beginning of the eighteenth century. For some time the bobbin meshes were made in haphazard directions and were rather irregular in size, as in Plates 56*b*, 59 and 60, but gradually they became more even and well controlled (Plate 52*b*).

Types overlapped, so it must not be supposed that laces can be closely dated by the particular style of ground alone. At first Flemish and Dutch workers seem to have used mesh grounds more frequently than the Italians – perhaps the style was first devised somewhere in the Netherlands – but the bride ground was also continued in Flanders for a long time. Some exquisite Brussels bobbin lace was still being made with very fine brides for many years into the eighteenth century, while an increasing quantity had the Brussels réseau. To distinguish between them, the laces are described as *Brussels à brides* or *à réseau*. Sometimes both grounds were used in one piece of lace. The overall tendency was for the fabric of lace to become lighter, with a more even texture, and for it to be worn more fully gathered. Before this was possible it needed the sort of unity given by a close ground, not the uneven texture of solid work and large open spaces. Bobbin lace led the way in this development and to the styles of the eighteenth century.

The three flounces of Brussels lace, Plates 61, 62 and 63, must date from about 1700. They were skilfully made of fine thread, particularly the first which may be from a little before 1700, and the last, probably made early in the eighteenth century. The designs of these flounces are

Plate 61   Flounce of Bobbin Lace with Arms of the Holy Roman Empire, Brussels, c. 1700. Width 32.5 cm.

typical of Brussels work of this time, inspired by the French style but more full and bold in the scale of their motifs. They are a free development of the style, admirably suited to this graceful bobbin lace with its soft and even texture.

The history of the flounce in Plate 61 is an intriguing unsolved mystery. It must have been ordered to celebrate the birth of a child, one of whose parents was a Hapsburg and the other a member of one of the German Electoral families. The cupid to the left holds a ribbon supporting a shield with the double-headed Hapsburg Eagle under the Imperial Crown, and the cupid on the right supports an Electoral Bonnet; but alas, in every repeat of the design, the shield that should be beneath it has been cut out and replaced by a flower from another part of the same lace. Under the canopy, which is only partly shown at the sides of the illustration, the lower part of a cradle standing on a dais remains, but the baby who must have lain in it has also been removed. What could have made the Hapsburgs, who evidently retained this lace, so dislike even the memory of this marriage and the poor child?

Gold and Silver Lace

Genoa and Spain were both famous for these very rich laces in the seventeenth century, but some of the so-called Point d'Espagne was made in France, in or near Paris, with the encouragement of Colbert. They were usually called Genoese Point and Spanish Point, although they were bobbin-made; the word *point*, meaning 'stitch', should really only be used for needle-made lace, but it has quite often also been used to suggest fineness or, as in this case, high quality. Metal lace was never very fine –

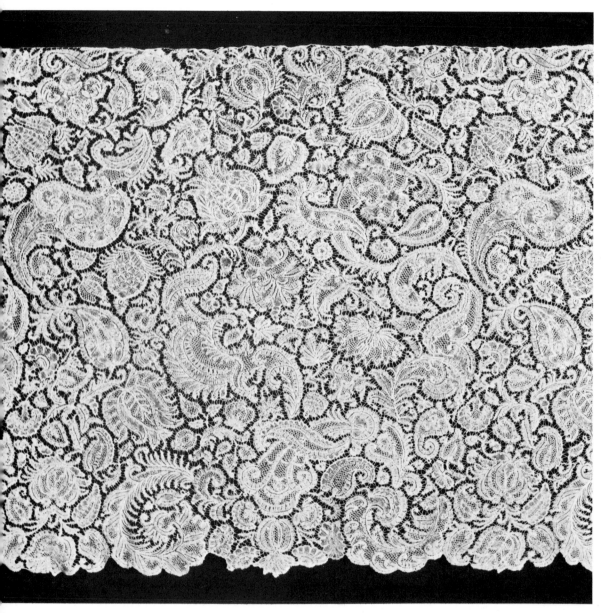

Plate 62   Deep Flounce of Bobbin Lace, Brussels, c. 1715. Width 60 cm.

it was impossible to bend and twist the stiffer threads as closely as linen, and the threads themselves were comparatively coarse; usually they were made by twisting a fine wire or metal strip round a silk thread. Silver gilt is nearly always used instead of pure gold.

The border, Plate 64, is Spanish, probably made early in the second half of the seventeenth century. There is a slight Moorish influence in the design, as there is in so much early Spanish work. The lace is made largely of silk threads covered with strips of silver and silver gilt, but also includes a continuous narrow horizontal band of parchment wound with gold wire; other strips of parchment that were once covered with black silk thread were worked into the design, but this silk has now almost entirely disappeared, leaving the light parchment showing. The dye has rotted it, as the early type of black dye always did. Only a few threads are left, protected by the folding and wrinkling of the parchment, but they are so weak that they crumble to dust at a touch. With the contrast of the black, gold and silver, as it was made, this splendid lace must have looked even more characteristically Spanish. Lace including parchment strips, known as *cartisane* lace, was made as early as the sixteenth century.

Some of the later history of this particular piece of lace is known. Louis XV's unmarried daughter, Madame Louise, entered a convent, the Carmel of Saint Denis, in 1769 and took this lace with her as a gift to the church. The convent was disbanded during the French Revolution, after the death of Madame Louise, and one of the nuns brought it to England to the convent she joined. It remained there until it was sold recently. The earlier part of its history is not known, but when the Spanish Infanta Maria

Plate 63   Deep Flounce of Bobbin Lace, Brussels, c. 1710–15. Width 65 cm.

Theresa travelled to France in 1660 to marry Louis XIV, seventy-five mules carried her Spanish fabrics and luxuries. Was this lace in one of those loads? The date would be just about right for the style of the lace.

By French standards, the Spanish were old-fashioned in their dress. They tended to look back to the sixteenth century, the time of Spain's glory and power. The French on the other hand were rising under Louis XIV to one of their greatest periods, and confidently looked forward. The meeting of Philip IV of Spain and Louis before the marriage showed the great contrast in court clothes, and influenced the Spaniards to move towards the later fashions. The French also paid the Spanish a compliment by adopting for a while their fashion for black silk lace, but not to the exclusion of the usual white linen work. The unfortunate dye has destroyed all this black lace, and that of the eighteenth century. The earliest we now have is from the nineteenth century, and nearly all of that from the middle and later part when new and safer black dyes were used.

In the second half of the seventeenth century, gold lace like that in Plate 64 and also in narrower widths was sewn smoothly over the silk of dresses, round the skirts, not necessarily right at the bottom, but following the shape of the garment, and perhaps up the front. It could be applied to men's coats in the same way, like a rich braid. Near the end of the century, from about 1685, ladies' dresses had an almost upholstered look, with heavy enrichment of tassels and fringes, braids and gold lace around the lower half of the skirt.

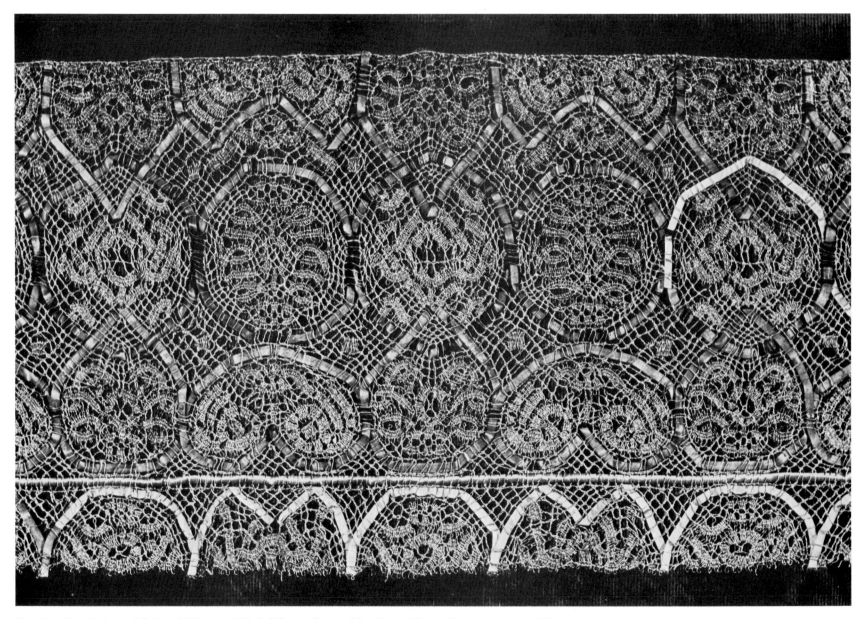

Plate 64   Spanish Lace of Gold and Silver, and Black Silk over Strips of Parchment, 'Point d'Espagne', c. 1660. Width 17.5 cm.

IV.   The Eighteenth Century – Baroque to Rococo, and the Classical Revival

All really high quality lace of the eighteenth century had exquisitely delicate texture. The extreme fineness and smoothness of the best linen thread was almost incredible. It was even finer than that used in the late seventeenth century for Point de Neige and Point de France, and was never equalled in later times.

The style of the design, however, changed profoundly during the century, from subtle richness to light and elegant gaiety and at the end to prettiness and delicate charm. There were no sudden breaks or surprises; it was a gradual change moving always in the same direction and affecting needlepoint and bobbin lace equally. It might have passed almost unnoticed as it happened year by year, but the difference between the work of 1700 and 1800 is very great and obvious.

In the early part of the century lace was boldly designed in the late baroque style that had developed towards the end of the seventeenth century. This is illustrated by the flounces shown in Plates 61, 62 and 63 that were described in the previous chapter. Their fine texture allowed them to be gathered softly and beautifully, and that is the way in which they were used. These were important pieces, but narrow borders of lace and lappets a few inches wide had the same qualities; the motifs finely drawn, the rhythm rich and the whole composition strong and just as carefully considered (Plates 82 and 83). The element of grandeur combined with delicacy

and lightness is fascinating, and not seen in many crafts.

As the century proceeded the scale of the designs was gradually reduced, just as it had been during the second half of the seventeenth century, but the effect was different. As the motifs became smaller they were not crowded more closely together as they had been in the previous century, but were displayed against larger areas of mesh. Throughout the eighteenth century, both for needlepoint and bobbin lace, the date can be judged approximately by the proportion of the design to the ground; the smaller or thinner the design and the larger the amount of réseau, the later the lace.

Before the middle of the century the designs had lost the full and robust quality that is essentially baroque, and had slipped gently into the rococo style: light, graceful and elegant. The delicate sprays of flowers crossed and balanced an undulating ribbon-like form around which the design grew (Plates 69a and 88). There were an infinite number of variations and enrichments of this theme. It is a style that demanded extraordinary skill of the designer – that he should hide his art, and seem only to have scattered his flowers and his ribbons for them to drop into their places and achieve a carefree perfection of their own accord. The mesh grounds used with these designs, and those that follow in the later part of the eighteenth century, were fine, light and even, so that

the elaborate patterns showed plainly against them.

Rococo designs continued for a long time after the middle of the century, but they were gradually weakened by the repetition of similar ideas. Thin wavering lines replaced the broad curves, and small sprigs of flowers were scattered to fill spaces, rather than being an essential part of the composition. The crossing undulating forms that originally occupied the whole breadth of the lace were normally used just as a narrow edging (Plate 70).

The Classical Revival in architecture and many branches of art was an important movement during the second half of the century, but it had little effect on lace design until near the end of the century. The controlled and formal character of the style was not sympathetic to the soft and luxurious nature of lace, and the rather thin late versions of rococo design continued till about the 1780s. There were, however, some pieces made in that decade that do show the classical influence. The flounce in Plate 91 includes a mixture of rococo and classical forms. It is Brussels work, in the Louis Seize tradition.

For the last fifteen or twenty years of the century fashion turned away from rich brocades to plainer silks. Finally in the 1790s women wore simple muslin dresses in the classical style. Lace was required to do nothing more for them than make a few soft and pretty frills, and even these were often of plain muslin. As the dresses them-

Plate 65 Baby's Christening Cap, with Holy Point Panel and Valenciennes Bobbin Lace Edging, English. Early eighteenth century. Length of Holy Point Panel 8 cm.

selves were very frequently white, a coloured silk ribbon was a more exciting accessory than white lace. At about this time, men stopped wearing lace altogether, a major tragedy for the lace industry everywhere. During this difficult period, design was influenced not only by classical forms but also by the great desire for simplicity. Such pattern as remained was concentrated on the edge of the lace, which was the only part that showed very much when the lace was closely gathered. Usually this was a border of little sprays of flowers and leaves, or single flower heads (Plate 75). A more classical design with the Greek anthemium as its motif is shown in Plate 92a. The rest of the lace, which was very fine in texture, was often powdered with tiny flowers or dots.

The French Revolution had an absolutely disastrous effect on the country's lace production and trade. During the Terror it was dangerous even to be well dressed. Aristocrats were in no position to patronize any industry, and those who had served them, particularly with luxuries such as lace, were in danger for that alone, and many were executed. The industry completely collapsed. Napoleon and later rulers encouraged revivals, but France never fully regained the importance it had enjoyed in this industry from the late seventeenth century to the Revolution.

Needlepoint Lace

Holy Point, spelt sometimes 'Holie' or 'Hollie', was a needlepoint lace which seems only to have been made in England, although it is just like the filling of seventeenth century Venetian Point. Plate 65 shows an early eighteenth century baby's cap with a panel of this lace; it was used especially to trim babies' christening

Plate 66 *Two Borders of Point de Venise à Réseau*   *a c. 1710. Width 6 cm.*   *b c. 1720–30. Width 10 cm.*

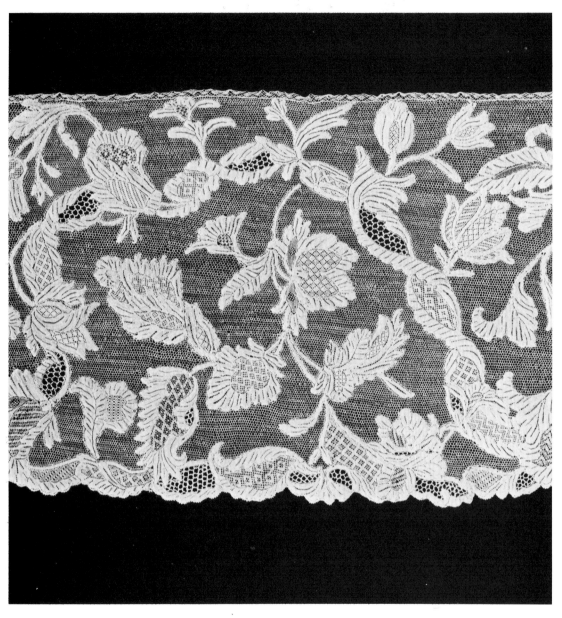

Plate 67   Point de Venise à Réseau. c. 1745–50. Width 22.5 cm.

clothes, and was also included on some samplers. The examples that now exist are nearly all from the eighteenth century, but there are earlier references, and the formal designs do suggest a tradition from the seventeenth century. The designs often include a dove, a crown, various flowers, and also the initials of the baby and sometimes the date. The bobbin lace edging of this cap, which appears to be original, is Valenciennes of about 1730 or 1740.

The borders on Plates 66 and 67 are of Venetian Point à Réseau, also known as Grounded Venetian Point. This is a flat lace, with the lower edge so very slightly accentuated that it could not really be described as a cordonnet. Those in Plate 66 were made very early in the eighteenth century and are in the baroque style; 66a still shows the seventeenth century Venetian tradition of design, 66b is more French in style. The third border on Plate 67 is later, of about 1745–50, and has a rococo design which is strongly influenced by French work. They all have a needle-made mesh ground similar to that developed at Alençon early in the eighteenth century, but in this Venetian lace it was always made in horizontal rows. At Alençon it was worked across the narrow width of the lace. Grounded Point was the last important Venetian lace. Later in the century only indifferent copies of French laces were made, and the quality of the workmanship declined steadily. At Burano, an island near Venice, the poor uneven thread used late in the eighteenth and early in the nineteenth century produced an unfortunate patchy and clouded effect in the mesh grounds.

The style of the designs of the two great eighteenth century French needlepoint laces, Alençon and Argentan, that developed from

Plate 68a   Argentan Needlepoint Lace, showing transition from Point de France, c. 1710–20. Width 6 cm.

Plate 68b   Argentella Needlepoint, made in France or possibly Venice, c. 1710–25. Width 6.5 cm.

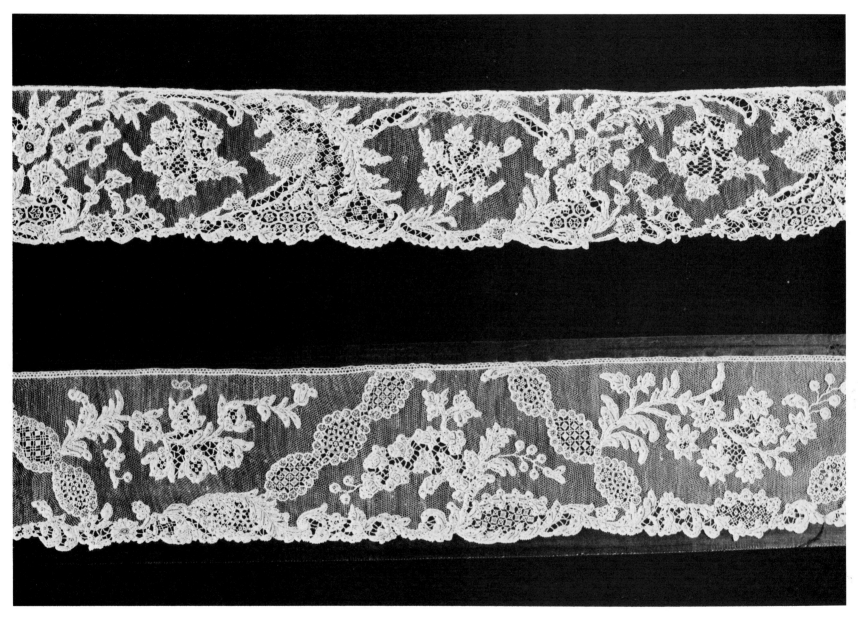

Plate 69   Alençon Needlepoint Lace.   a   c. 1740–50. Width 8 cm.   b   c. 1750–55. Width 9 cm.

Plate 70   Alençon Needlepoint Lace.   a Border, c. 1750–60. Width 8.5 cm.   b Lappet, c. 1765–70. Width 11.5 to 9.5 cm; complete length 59 cm.

Plate 71a   Argentan Lace Cap, with Alençon Border, c. 1755. 25 × 33 cm.

Plate 71b   Argentan Border, c. 1760–65. Width 7 cm.

Point de France, were very similar to each other. They are shown in their approximate chronological order in Plates 68 to 75. Point de France continued from the late seventeenth into the first years of the eighteenth century with small brides, decorated with picots, making its slightly irregular ground, but by about 1710 this was being reduced to the scale of a mesh. Needlepoint lace was following the lead of bobbin lace to a more even texture.

The réseau adopted at Alençon, the original home of Point de France, was a mesh of open buttonhole stitches, each with an extra twist, worked in rows across the lace with the thread taken back and twisted through the loops of each row of stitches before the next row was made. This pulled the stitches into a more square shape than the natural form of buttonholing (Plate 129b). The lace-makers of the neighbouring town of Argentan, about twenty miles away, used a stronger réseau that was more like the Point de France ground but a lot smaller. The border on Plate 68a is very early Argentan; its mesh is buttonholed over, without the picots of the Point de France ground, but it is not as regular, or as close, as it was to become. It shows the transition from Point de France. The fully developed Argentan ground was a regular hexagonal mesh, buttonholed over with tiny stitches. At first sight it looks coarser than the Alençon réseau, but it is really much closer work. Each side of the hexagon has from five to ten covering stitches (Plate 130a). Late in the eighteenth and in the nineteenth century a new and less laborious version of this ground was used, called *bride tortillée*. Instead of buttonholing over the hexagons, a thread was just twisted round them. The effect was less sharp and clear as the angles were blurred by the continuous twisting thread.

Plate 72 Argentan Lace, c. 1765–75. Width 16 cm.

Plates 74 and 75a are of lace with this ground, but it cannot be distinguished in a photograph. It is sometimes necessary, when examining the actual lace, to use a magnifying glass. The smaller mesh at the edge of the border is the normal Alençon réseau, but for these narrow edges was worked horizontally. Lace with this quicker and cheaper ground was also made at Alençon. Workers from the two towns are known to have moved from one to the other. In both Alençon and Argentan lace the motifs and the edge were emphasized by buttonholed cordonnets.

Plate 68b is a variant of Argentan lace known as Argentella. Instead of the usual mesh it has a patterned ground of rather large and somewhat irregular hexagons, with small solid hexagons within them. Sometimes other rich grounds were used, but the small solid hexagons seem typical. This type of lace was almost certainly made at Argentan and may also have been made by the Venetians, copying the French style. Some consider that it was made in Genoa as well, although the principal products of that city were bobbin lace, and gold and silver laces.

The gathered lace, Plate 73, is a shaped sleeve frill. These were made of needlepoint or bobbin lace, in sets to be worn two or three deep, graduated in width. Each frill was also shaped to pass over the arm as a narrow border and fall in a deeper flounce behind the elbow. They were known as *engageantes*. This most graceful fashion lasted from about 1690 to 1780.

Alençon and Argentan were considered to be 'winter laces' by fashionable society in the eighteenth century. Although they were light in weight and delicate in design, they still had the firm and crisp texture of needlepoint lace which was thought to be more suitable for use with richer colours and heavier materials. The ex-tremely fine and soft bobbin laces of Flanders and France were chosen for the lighter silks of summer.

Most of the lace made at Brussels was bobbin-made, but in the eighteenth century they also produced some particularly delicate needle-point. It was similar in style to the contemporary Alençon lace, but in the earlier specimens the design was often slightly larger in scale. It was always more lightly made than Alençon; the stitches forming the toilé were not pulled up as closely, and the cordonnet was formed of just a very few threads thinly buttonholed over with spaced-out stitches, not tightly and closely as in the French lace. The thread used was amazingly fine, so the total effect was lighter and more filmy. Very little of this lace has survived; it was more fragile than Alençon, and probably much less was made. Plate 76 shows two lappets of about 1750 and 1780, both with the pattern in this needlepoint lace and the ground in the fine Brussels bobbin réseau, worked around the motifs. The earlier one, with quite a large proportion of the needle-made lace, shows the difference of texture if it is compared with the Alençon sleeve frill in Plate 73.

The next three plates are of muslin embroidery. It was quite often professional work, but sometimes done by ladies for their own use to take the place of lace they perhaps could not afford. It copied from lace the idea of a solid design against an open ground by using white embroidery on as fine a muslin as possible. The delicate fillings, which look like those of lace, were sometimes drawn thread work, but often the muslin threads were only pulled aside by the stitches. The solid white was emphasized by different techniques. For the sleeve frill, Plate 77a, the outlines were worked through double

Plate 73 Alençon Shaped Sleeve Frill, c. 1765–75. Greatest width 20.5 cm.

Plate 74   Argentan or Alençon Kerchief, with Bride Tortillée Ground, c. 1780. 130 cm × 55 cm.

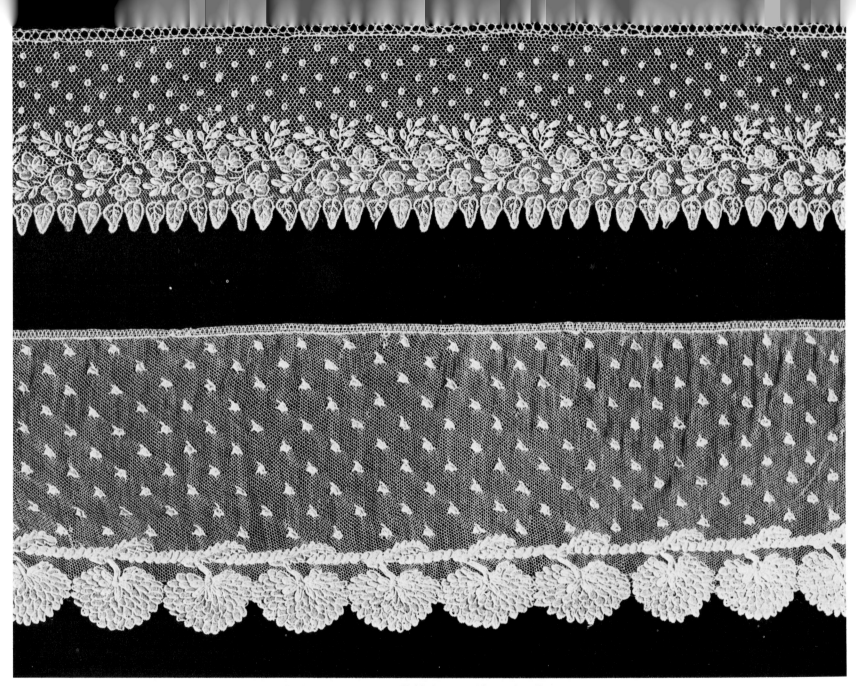

Plate 75a   Argentan or Alençon Border, with Bride Tortillée Ground, c. 1785-90. Width 8 cm.   *Plate 75b   Alençon Border, c. 1785-90. Width 10.5 cm.*

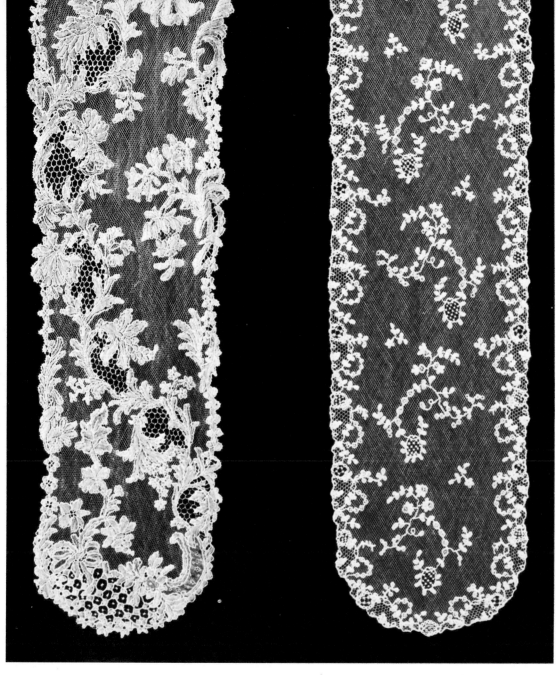

muslin. The back layer was then cut away except for those areas that were intended to be the whitest, and the fillings were worked on the single remaining layer of muslin. In the fragment of a sleeve frill, Plate 77*b*, the effect was produced by embroidery on the underside of the muslin increasing its density. On the other hand, the white design was embroidered on the right side of both the triangular shawl, Plate 78, and the apron, part of which is shown on Plate 79. Muslin embroideries were made from the early eighteenth century and right through the nineteenth century. The early muslin, being hand woven from hand-spun cotton, always has the cloudy appearance of these specimens.

Bobbin Lace

The designs of eighteenth century bobbin lace follow the changes of style already described, and the plates of this group are arranged to show this development and some comparisons between certain types, rather than in groups according to the places in which they were made. Plates 81 and 82 show the changes in the shape of lappets from the square-ended one of the late seventeenth century, Plate 81*a*, to slightly rounded corners at the very beginning of the eighteenth century, Plate 82*a*, and those with rounded ends and shaped sides that became fashionable in the 1720s, shown in Plates 81*b* and 82*b*.

There are two basic techniques for making bobbin lace, which can emphasize different characteristics of the designs. Workers specialized in one or the other, and usually the lace of each district was all of the type that had become traditional in that place. They also adopted particular mesh grounds by which their various

Plate 76   Lappets of Brussels Needlepoint on Bobbin-made Grounds.
a   c. 1745–50. Width 10 to 8 cm; complete length 60 cm.   b   c. 1780. Width 10 to 8.5 cm; complete length 82 cm.

Plate 77   Embroidered Muslin.   *a Sleeve Frill, Worked on Double and Single Muslin, c. 1730–40. Depth of embroidery 10.5 cm.*
b Part of a Sleeve Frill, Worked on Single Muslin, c. 1730–40. Depth 10 cm.

Plate 78   Embroidered Muslin Kerchief, c. 1745. 123×39 cm.

laces can be recognized, although some grounds were used in several different lace-making centres. In the nineteenth century the whole tradition of specialization broke down, and every fashionable lace was copied in other towns and other countries, but usually retained the name of the place in which it originated.

In one of the techniques, 'straight lace' or *fil continu*, the same threads carry right through the lace and form the solid clothwork, the mesh ground and the fillings as the work progresses. The threads lie approximately parallel with the sides of the lace or cross it at right angles. The elaboration of fillings and the shaping of the lower edge prevent this from being exact, but it is true of the general effect. This technique, which was used in the laces of Binche, Valenciennes, Mechlin, Lille and others, demonstrates the relationship of bobbin lace-making to weaving (Plates 84*a* and 85). It gives great unity to the fabric, and when used with the early eighteenth century style of rich designs that fill the surface very closely, set against intricate réseaux of nearly the same weight, it produces extraordinarily subtle laces. They can almost look like extremely fine muslin from a little distance, yet they have most beautiful designs with exquisitely rich detail, to be enjoyed almost in secret (Plate 82*a*). By the middle of the century, when the areas of plain mesh had increased, the less remarkable but nevertheless charming designs could be seen at a glance.

In making any straight lace the same threads passed from the clothwork into the mesh and into the clothwork again, as required. When the mesh was strong, as in Valenciennes where it was made of plaits of four strands, there were plenty of threads available to form a closely woven clothwork like fine lawn (Plate 86*b*).

When the mesh was delicate, as in Lille, there were fewer threads and the clothwork was light and open. The motifs then needed an outline of thicker thread, known as 'gimp', to give better definition (Plate 132b).

In lace made by the other technique, 'pieced lace', the pattern was formed first, by itself, with the threads following the curves of the design in whatever direction they led. The ground of brides or mesh was then worked round the completed design, the extra threads being hooked into the edges of the clothwork of the pattern. Brussels lace was the most important of this type in the eighteenth century, and probably the most important of all bobbin laces at this time. The technically less complicated seventeenth century Italian and Flemish bobbin lace described in Chapter III, with designs of continuous braid-like forms joined by added brides, also belong to this group. The rhythm of design was emphasized by the pieced lace technique, by the direction of the threads, and in the case of Brussels lace by cordonnets made on the edge of the clothwork (Plate 131a).

The two types are shown together on Plate 84; Binche, the straight lace, 84a; and Brussels, the pieced lace, 84b. Both are very fine quality borders of the early eighteenth century. This sort of Brussels lace was known as *Point d'Angleterre*, a deceptive name used to aid the continuous and very extensive smuggling that evaded the English prohibition of the import of foreign lace. The fact that lace was being made in Devonshire by the same process as that

Plate 79 *Embroidered Muslin Apron, c. 1765–75. Complete apron 118 cm wide × 96 cm deep; Basket of Flowers 13 cm high.*

Plate 80   Bobbin Lace.   *a Binche, End of seventeenth century. Width 7 cm.*
b Flemish Border, matching the Lappet on Plate 52b, c. 1695–1700. Width 7.5 cm.

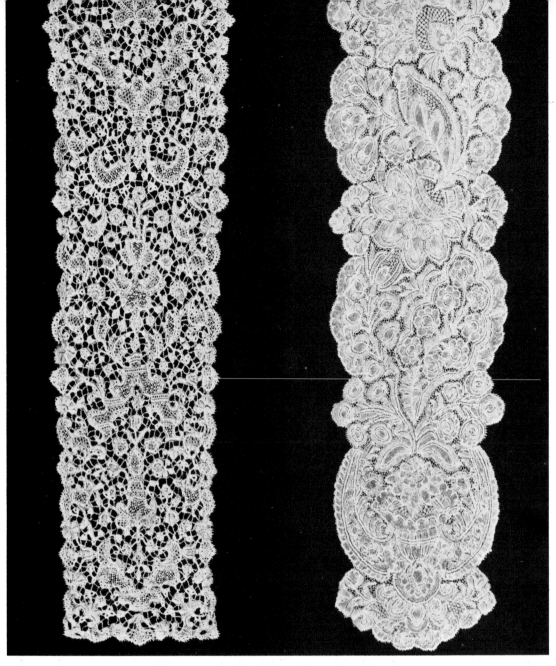

used in Brussels, and with the same mesh, helped the pretence that the smuggled Point d'Angleterre had been made in England. Plate 84c shows a typical narrow border of this Devonshire work, which in truth could not have been confused with the superb lace of Brussels in design or workmanship.

Further examples of early eighteenth century Brussels are the cap, Plate 83, and its matching lappet, Plate 82b. They have the fine bride ground which was still often used at this time. When the design was as rich and full as in these pieces there was not enough space between motifs for the regular pattern of a mesh ground to be developed. A 'Brussels Head', meaning a cap and pair of lappets, of this quality cost at least forty pounds in Queen Anne's time. The linen thread used for lace like this was the finest possible, and to preserve its elasticity it was spun in a dim light and damp atmosphere, with just a ray of light on the thread itself. It was claimed that Brussels thread was the finest of all, but that used at Binche, Valenciennes and Mechlin at this time was of very nearly the same standard.

Plate 90a shows the Brussels mesh ground used in a border of about 1765, with a few brides and a fancy filling for variety. The Brussels mesh was hexagonal, with four sides formed by twisting two threads and the other two sides by plaiting four threads. Under the organized system of lace-making at Brussels the work was divided up amongst specialist workers, and the beauty of the completed lace was dependent on their strict adherance to the properly planned designs which were normally of an extremely high standard. This particular border was probably made by some isolated workers, outside any organized group. It has a rather unsatisfactory design; the pattern at the edge wavers in an in-

Plate 81   *Flemish Bobbin-made Lappets.*
    a Designed in the style of Point de France, c. 1700. Width 11 to 9 cm; complete length 58 cm.
    b Brussels Lappet, c. 1725–35. Width 10.5 to 9 cm; complete length 62 cm.

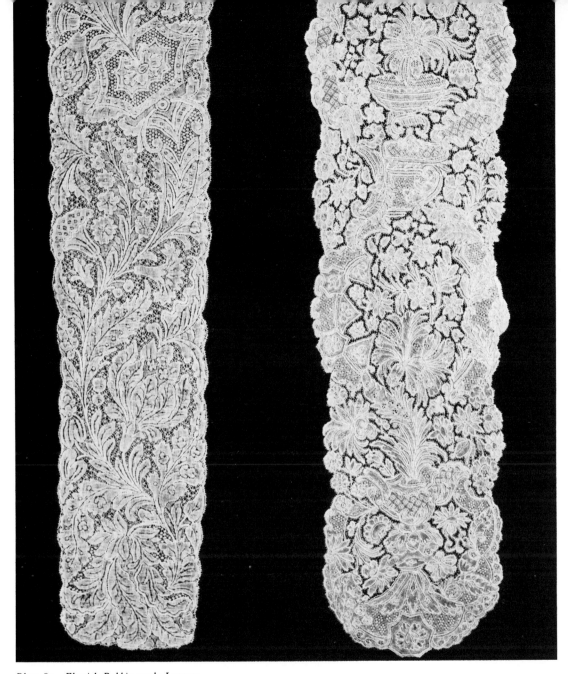

Plate 82   Flemish Bobbin-made Lappets.
   a Mechlin, c. 1710–15. Width 10 to 7.5 cm; complete length 57 cm.
   b Brussels, matching the Cap on Plate 83, c. 1725–30. Width 12 to 9.5 cm; complete length 59 cm.

consequent way, and the sprays are squeezed uncomfortably in the upper part; the one to the left of the centre looks suspiciously as if it were originally designed as two sprigs that have been joined together with an odd flower and leaf.

Towards the end of the century the reduction in the scale of the motifs and the consequent growing importance of the réseau led to a variation in the technique of Brussels work. The flounce of Louis Seize style in Plate 91, the border in Plate 92a and the veil, Plate 111, each have a complete ground of the usual mesh, made in narrow strips about 1.5 centimetres wide and joined almost imperceptibly to make the required area. This all-over ground is often referred to as *drochel* or *vrai drochel* to distinguish it from the machine-made net commonly used in the nineteenth century. The separately made motifs of the design were sewn on to the ground, which from the back of the lace can be seen continuing behind them. In the earlier work the mesh was constructed in position between the motifs, and therefore did not pass behind them, although to avoid cutting threads little plaits were often taken across the back from one area of mesh to the next.

Binche and Valenciennes were very similar to each other in the early part of the century. Both were of the straight lace type, made of very fine thread and using a great variety of fancy fillings. Binche sometimes had no plain mesh at all, the ground being entirely made of the more elaborate fillings, and on the whole was slightly more open in texture than Valenciennes (Plates 84a and 85). It is so light and delicate that it practically seems to disappear in water when it is being washed; it looks almost like a floating milky film. Brussels was made of just as fine a thread – perhaps sometimes even finer – but the lace has a

Plate 83   Brussels Bobbin Lace Cap, with Valenciennes Edging, c. 1725–30. 25 × 28.5 cm.

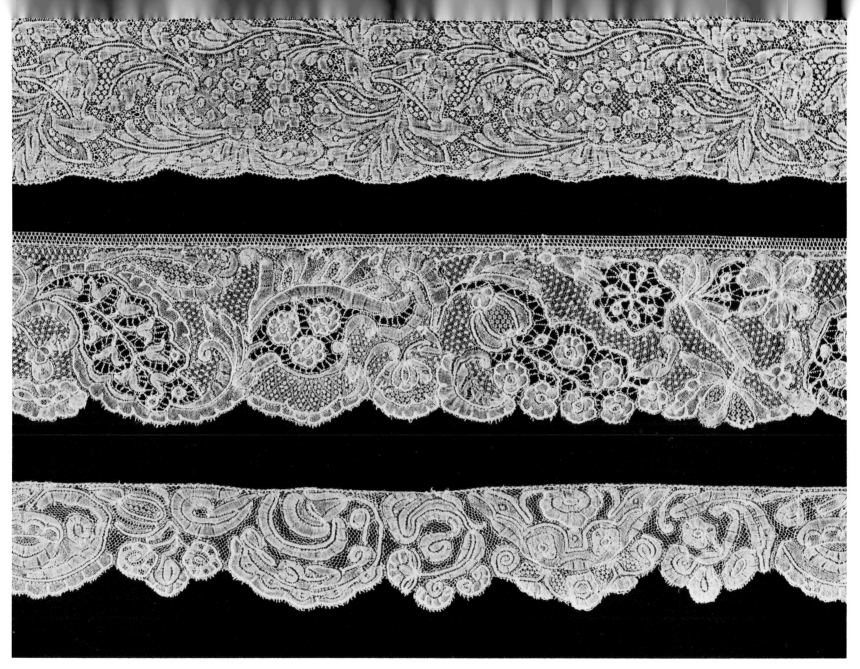

Plate 84 Bobbin-made Lace Borders.   *a Binche, c. 1710–20. Width 5.5 cm.*   *b Brussels, c. 1725–35. Width 6.5 cm.*   *c Devonshire, c. 1765–80. Width 4.3 cm.*

Plate 85   Bobbin Lace Borders.   a Binche or Valenciennes, c. 1725–35. Width 5 cm.   b Binche, c. 1710–20. Width 6.5 cm.   c Valenciennes, c. 1740. Width 7 cm.

Plate 86 Bobbin Lace.   a Mechlin, c. 1740. Width 7 cm.   b Valenciennes with Round Mesh, c. 1750–55. Width 7 cm.   c Valenciennes with 'Cinq Trous' Mesh, c. 1745. Width 8 cm.

Plate 87a *Mechlin Cap, with Valenciennes Edging, c. 1745–50. 23 × 27 cm.*
Plate 87b *Binche, c. 1725. Width 3 cm.*

little more substance with its cordonnets and slightly closer work. In the early eighteenth century Valenciennes usually had some plain ground as well as the rich fillings; this was a réseau traditionally used in seventeenth century Flemish lace, known as *cinq trous* because there were five tiny holes in the plaited work between the larger holes of the mesh (Plate 132a). Later a different and rather solid plaited ground with round holes was adopted and used without the fancy fillings, or with only small areas of them. It was known as the 'Valenciennes round mesh'. With this ground the toilé also became closer, and before the middle of the century it was like a fine smoothly woven linen (Plate 86b).

The terms *Vraie Valenciennes* and *Fausse Valenciennes* were used in the eighteenth century, but their meaning is not really clear. It may be that *vraie* meant lace with the regular round mesh that was recognized as belonging to this lace, and *fausse*, lace with the earlier grounds that were not especially associated with Valenciennes; or that *vraie* meant the lace made in the town itself, and *fausse*, lace made in the surrounding country. The former alternative seems the more likely, as Madame du Barry's accounts show that she bought both sorts, and she probably wanted the best available of its type. Country-made lace was usually inferior to that made in the central town of a lace-making district.

In the nineteenth century, when Valenciennes lace was made at Ypres and Bruges, a diamond-shaped mesh was used, the sides of which were formed of four thread plaits. Both the round and diamond réseaux were strong, and the laces were called *Les Eternelles Valenciennes*. It was also expensive lace, as the work was very slow; it took a professional full-time

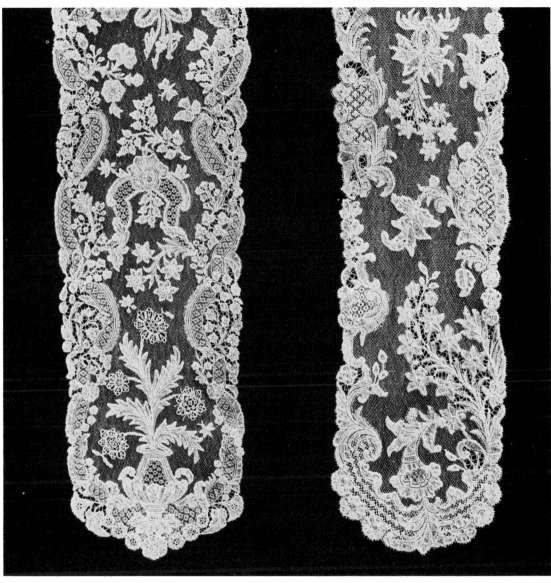

Plate 88   Brussels Lappets in Rococo Style, with Brussels Mesh Grounds.
a Bobbin-made with Needlepoint Flowers on the lowest spray, c. 1745–50. Width 12 to 9 cm; complete length 59 cm.
b Bobbin-made, c. 1750–55. Width 10.5 to 9 cm; length 60 cm.

worker ten months to make a pair of men's sleeve ruffles, and three to four hundred bobbins would be needed for a fine lace about seven centimetres wide.

Both Valenciennes and Lille were Flemish towns until the late seventeenth century, but they passed to France by treaties in 1668 and 1678. Binche, less than thirty miles from Valenciennes, was left on the Flemish side of the new frontier. The similarity of Valenciennes and Binche lace in the early eighteenth century show that the lace-making tradition of the district was not broken.

Lace had probably been made at Lille since the late sixteenth century, but a distinctive type was not produced until the late eighteenth century, when a light and simple straight lace became known as 'Lille'. It had a clear, delicate ground made of only two twisted threads and the rather slight patterns were outlined with gimp. The designs were in the general late eighteenth century style, mostly concentrated along the edge of the lace, and the ground was sometimes decorated with small square dots. A border is shown in Plate 117a. It was comparatively quick to make, and therefore cheaper than many, and was popular for summer wear both in the late eighteenth and during the first half of the nineteenth century. Lace of a similar type, with the same ground, was made in the English East Midlands during this period and later. The designs were rather broader than those of Lille, and were enriched with various bold decorative fillings: honeycomb, mayflower and others. This lace is called 'Buckinghamshire Point', though it is of course a bobbin lace (Plates 117b and 119a).

The town of Mechlin, or Malines, only fifteen miles from Antwerp and less from Brussels, was

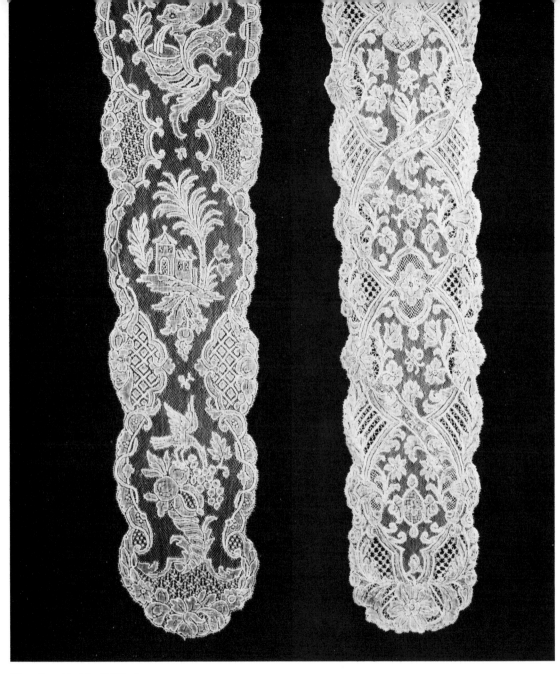

Plate 89 *Mechlin Bobbin Lappets.*
a c. 1755–60. Width 10.5 to 8.5 cm; complete length 56 cm.
b c. 1750–60. Width 10.5 to 8.5 cm; complete length 55 cm.

one of the most important centres of lace-making in Flanders, and among bobbin laces of the eighteenth century Mechlin was second only to Brussels. It was fine and costly, and a favourite at the courts of Europe as a summer lace when Alençon and Argentan, with their firmer texture, were considered to be winter laces. In 1713 Queen Anne bought eighty-three yards of Mechlin for £247.6s.9d. A good worker could make only about two and a quarter inches a day.

Mechlin was of the fil continu, or straight lace, type. The clothwork was not as close as that of typical Valenciennes after its round mesh had been developed, and Mechlin thread was very fine, so a thicker thread was used as an outline to give definition to the design. This thread has a silky appearance, but is linen, loosely spun so that the fibres lie nearly parallel with each other and show their natural sheen.

At the beginning of the eighteenth century, before Mechlin had developed its characteristic réseau, it looked very like Binche or the earliest Valenciennes. It had much the same light texture and full rich style of design covering nearly the whole surface. The small areas of ground in between were sometimes filled with elaborate patterns just as in Binche, or with the cinq trous ground used in Valenciennes before its own round mesh was adopted. The only difference was the outlining thread of Mechlin which at first was very delicate. The comparison between the Mechlin lappet, Plate 82a, and the Binche border, Plate 84a, is striking. All three laces were developing in the same artistic climate and from the earlier Flemish tradition.

The Mechlin mesh, which began to be used during the first quarter of the eighteenth century, was similar to that of Brussels – that is, hexagonal with two sides of four thread plaits

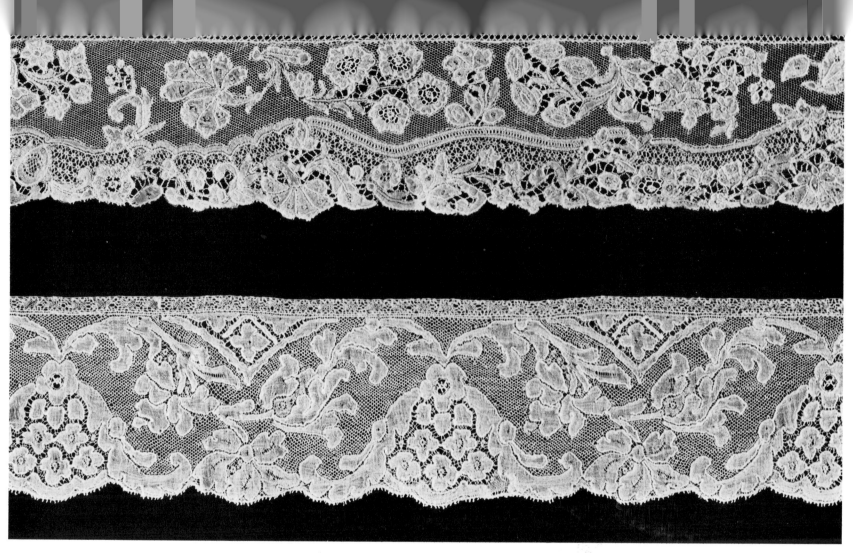

Plate 90   Bobbin Lace Borders.   a Brussels, c. 1765–70. Width 5.5 cm.   b Mechlin, c. 1750. Width 6 cm.

and four of two twisted threads – but the open holes of Mechlin were smaller than those of Brussels because the plaited sides were shorter. Plates 86*a* and 90*b* show borders, the earlier one having smaller areas of mesh than the later. Plates 87*a* and 89, of a cap and two separate lappets, show the designs passing from the formal and symmetrical to the rococo style. The straight-edged border, Plate 92*b*, belongs to the late Classical Revival period, although the vine and grape motifs, much used by the Romans, are here drawn in a naturalistic rather than a classical manner. These delicate borders were very fashionable for the soft frills of the period, and are the most characteristic lace of the end of the century.

Plate 91   Brussels Bobbin Flounce, with Design Applied to a Continuous Hand-made Ground, c. 1780–85. Width 40 cm.

Plate 92a   Brussels Border, c. 1785–90. Width 11 cm.   *Plate 92b   Mechlin Border, c. 1785–90. Width 9.5 cm.*

V. The Nineteenth Century – Hand-made Lace in the Machine Age

The beginning of the nineteenth century was a difficult time for the lace industry everywhere. France's trade was in ruins after the Revolution and practically all Europe was involved in the Napoleonic Wars. Within the industry's own affairs conditions were no more favourable, for when lace went out of fashion for men at the end of the eighteenth century, half its customers were permanently lost. The ladies did not abandon lace, but as long as the purely classical style of dress lasted, lace and trimmings were unimportant. At first their designs were limited to slight patterns, like those of the end of the previous century, that were pretty but of no great consequence. The gathered borders of Lille, Valenciennes and Mechlin were used as they had been in the late eighteenth century. However, the nineteenth century version of classical design in general was soon changed from the extreme delicacy that had been the ideal of the late eighteenth century, to a more grandiose Napoleonic desire for imperial splendour which influenced his enemies as much as his friends. The change was shown in heavier and even sometimes pompous architectural and furniture design, but was reflected less obviously, and more happily, in lace by giving renewed importance to the design and allowing it to spread again over the surface instead of being confined just to the edges. The Brussels veil, Plate 111, is an example of a wholly classical design of this period. Floral designs, which were always more

popular for lace, also gradually regained freedom and liveliness.

The lovely Brussels skirt of needlepoint appliqué on a hand-made bobbin ground, Plate 93, has a beautiful floral design, with the classical form of repeating verticals rising from a horizontal base. The illustration shows only the lower part, to give better detail; but on the whole skirt, which was designed for a high waistline, there is three times the length of vertical stripe, which gives a more classical proportion to the design. The upright edges met loosely at the front of the dress and curved away at the bottom to show the underskirt. It is a beautiful design, restrained but not timid, plainly showing the new vitality.

During the early part of the century, from about 1805, French silk Blonde lace was extremely fashionable. It is a very light and fragile bobbin lace made of fine natural creamy-coloured silk which could be used very prettily for light veils and frilled trimmings on the simple classical dresses (Plates 113 and 114). Black silk Chantilly lace was made in the same districts but was not especially fashionable, except in Spain, until the 1830s, when Blonde declined from favour and was replaced by Chantilly which remained one of the most fashionable laces until about 1870.

The earliest inventions of the Industrial Revolution to affect lace-making came near the end of the eighteenth century, when the first

machine-made nets were produced. They were made on adaptations of the stocking frame, but were rather unsatisfactory as they were very apt to pull out of shape and would unravel like knitting if a thread were broken. A better net was invented by John Heathcoat in 1809 and soon became very popular. It had a twisted hexagonal mesh more like a bobbin-made ground, and would not unravel. Designs were worked on the nets by hand in various embroidery techniques. Tambour work was done with a hook but looks like chain stitching; plain and fancy darning stitches were used for the type known as needle-run work, and fancy fillings as nearly as possible like lace fillings were added for enrichment. Plate 94 shows a delicate veil of tambour work.

Embroidered net was the height of fashion between about 1810 and 1830, but it continued to be worn through the nineteenth and into the twentieth century. In England it was chiefly made in Nottingham, but also in London, Coggleshall, the Isle of Wight and other places; from 1829 it was made at Limerick in Ireland and some was produced in Scotland. Machine net was also made in France from 1819, and fine embroidery was done at various centres there and in other countries. It was used for large pieces like veils, long scarves, cape collars and flounces by many who could only have afforded a little lace made entirely by hand. The cost of machine net was only a fraction of that of a hand-made ground, and it was further reduced

Plate 93   Brussels Needlepoint Appliqué on Vrai Drochel Ground, Skirt of a Lace Dress, c. 1825. Total length of skirt 108 cm; width 220 cm; depth of border 30 cm.

by the use of steam power from about 1820. Gradually through the century other mechanical improvements brought the cost of the cheapest quality down to a few coppers for a square yard. By about 1830 a new net with a diamond-shaped mesh began to replace the finer Heathcoat type, and became the most commonly used net. In the later part of the century machine chain stitching was used instead of tambour work for most of the embroidery. This does seem to be the point at which this lace must cease to be classed as hand-made.

Advances in machine products followed each other swiftly. Patterned and spotted nets were made in the 1820s and became common in the 1830s; and late in that decade the Jacquard process, originally intended for weaving patterned cloth, was applied to lace machines. In this process punched cards control the weaving mechanically and make complicated design a practical possibility for the machine. By the late 1830s and in the next decade quite good imitations of some hand-made laces were being produced, but in some cases, even as late as the 1850s, outlining threads had to be run round the patterns by hand. This is true of the remarkable copies of black silk Chantilly lace which, without close examination, are not easily distinguished from the hand-made lace. Valenciennes was also copied dangerously well later in the century.

Another use of machine-made net, perhaps even more important than as a ground for embroidery, was for appliqué lace. Brussels workers in the late eighteenth century had begun to use their own hand-made mesh as a ground on which to apply both bobbin and needlepoint motifs; the substitution of machine net, when it became available, was a very natural

91

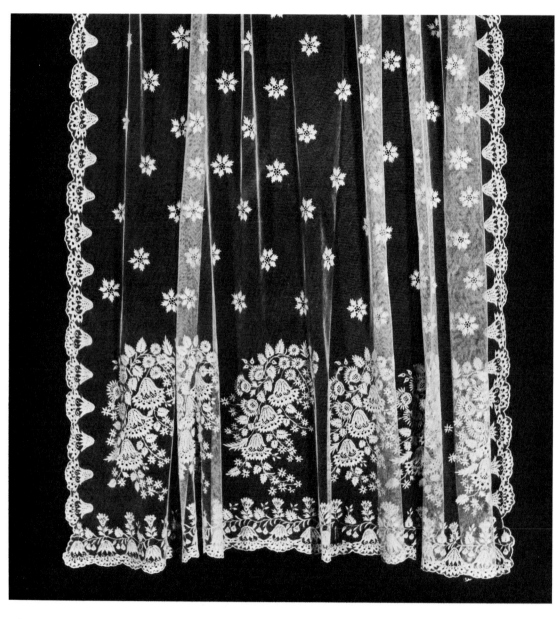

Plate 94   Veil, Tambour Embroidery on Machine Net Ground, English c. 1825. Width 115 cm; depth 93 cm.

development. By the 1830s this was common practice; it grew to be one of the favourite laces of the century and helped to bring prosperity back to the Brussels industry. The designs were at first quite light, with sprays of flowers arranged mainly near the edge of the lace, and often with small motifs strewn over the ground. Gradually, as the revival of rococo design became generally fashionable, in about 1840 and through the middle of the century, naturalistically drawn flowers were arranged in larger and more elaborate groups and swags, with ribbons and light scrolls (Plate 97). The edges of the lace that had been straight, or nearly so at the beginning of the century, were mostly of small scallops by about 1820, and broader ones as the patterns became larger and fuller. These tendencies in design affected all the fashionable laces.

The use of the Brussels hand-made ground for appliqué did not stop abruptly, but because of its great cost was used less and less frequently; by about 1850 it was made only for exhibition pieces and royal orders, and before the end of the century had died out completely. Appliqué on machine net remained popular and fashionable into the twentieth century, particularly for wedding veils and deep flounces. Honiton bobbin-made motifs were applied to the machine ground in just the same way as Brussels motifs, and both Queen Adelaide and Queen Victoria encouraged the Devonshire lace-workers by their patronage. In 1840 Queen Victoria's wedding dress was richly decorated with Honiton lace which cost £1000 at that time. This was not appliqué lace–it was made entirely by hand – but she also ordered pieces of appliqué at various times.

All the machine-made nets were woven of

Plate 95   Cape Collar, Embroidered Muslin, c. 1835. Depth of collar 27 cm; of embroidery 11.5 cm.

Plate 96   Alençon Needlepoint Border, c. 1850. Width 15 cm. Said to have been owned by the Empress Eugénie.

cotton, which was cheaper than linen and, being also machine spun, much cheaper than the traditional hand-spun linen lace thread. Many of the hand workers, struggling against the growing competition from the machines, were glad to be able to cut their prices by changing to cotton thread, and by about 1835 the great majority were using it. Those making the finest and most costly laces mainly continued to use either hand-spun or machine-spun linen. In the middle of the century the hand-spun linen could cost £240 a pound, or much more for the very finest thread, and the famous Flemish hand-spinning industry was dying out. On the whole the makers of the cheaper laces who tried to compete with machine prices by making quicker and coarser lace, were the worst hit, as their work was in the end no more attractive than that of the machine. Those who made the most expensive laces like Alençon and the best Brussels kept up their quality, and succeeded better by offering a more beautiful product than the machine could make, one that the wealthy were therefore willing to buy even at very high prices. Lace made entirely by hand was produced for them throughout the nineteenth century. The scale of this luxury industry was considerably reduced in the last quarter of the century by the continually increasing and improving manufacture of machine lace, although a

Plate 97   Flounce of Brussels Needlepoint Appliqúe on Machine Net, with relief on some flowers, c. 1850. Width 48 cm.

Plate 98   Brussels Point de Gaze Flounce, c. 1855–60. Width 16 cm.

Plate 99   Brussels Point de Gaze Flounce, with added petals in relief, c. 1860–65. Width 27 cm.

Plate 100   Brussels Needlepoint Appliqué on Machine Net, c. 1865–75. Width 72 cm.

Plate 101   Panel of Crochet, French, c. 1830–40. 38×33.5 cm.

great deal of that was used by people who would not have been able to afford the hand-made lace even if there had been no substitute available. There were in fact still a great many wealthy people, both of the old aristocratic families and of those who were making new riches by industry, who could afford expensive lace just as well as the aristocrats of earlier centuries.

Alençon needlepoint, made in the same way as it had been in the eighteenth century, was the most expensive of these laces and gained its position as the leading lace during the 1840s, being especially fashionable in France at the court of the Second Empire from 1852 to the fall of Napoleon III in 1870. The Empress Eugénie was the undoubted leader of fashion; she loved lace, and particularly Alençon and Chantilly, the two great French laces of the period.

The Alençon industry had been practically ruined by the French Revolution. Some workers struggled on and during the First Empire received important commissions and encouragement from Napoleon I. After his downfall in 1815, they were again in such a precarious position that many of them turned to muslin embroidery which was then very fashionable and in great demand. Needlepoint lace could never be fully appreciated in a period when simplicity and soft delicacy were more admired than richness, but the gradual change of fashion towards more elaborate design in the 1830s and 40s helped the revival of Alençon. The nineteenth century rococo was not just a copy of the more subtle rococo style of the eighteenth century, in which Alençon had produced such wonderful lace, but was a real expression of nineteenth century exuberance and had genuine character of

Plate 102   Panel of Furnishing Lacis, French, c. 1870. Width 45 cm.

its own. It was a style that could be sympathetically expressed in needlepoint lace, with its clear definition of design and firm texture (Plates 96 and 98). The designs were rich and beautifully drawn in a naturalistic manner, using effects of shading that were produced by the varying closeness of buttonhole stitching. The whole of the workmanship was remarkably skilful. Black Chantilly, which was one of the most fashionable bobbin laces from about 1840 to 1870, used this floral rococo style very beautifully. Worn over light colours, its fine black silk thread made a most delicate tracery (Plate 115).

Brussels *Point de Gaze*, a new needlepoint lace, was shown at the 1851 Crystal Palace Exhibition, and was immediately successful (Plates 98 and 99). It was an obvious competitor with Alençon for the exclusive market, but was somewhat less expensive, as it could be made rather more quickly. With its introduction Brussels became one of the most important centres for needlepoint lace in Europe, as well as continuing to hold its long established importance in bobbin lace-making. The fine needlepoint made there in the eighteenth century was more exquisite, but compared with Point de Gaze it had only been made in very small quantities. The designs of the new lace were very much in the same style as those of Alençon, and some were actually French. Perhaps, on the whole, Alençon designs were a little more controlled than those of Point de Gaze in which

Plate 103a   Knitted Doyley. Early nineteenth century. Diameter 23 cm.

Plate 103b   Knitted Border. Early nineteenth century. Width 15 cm.

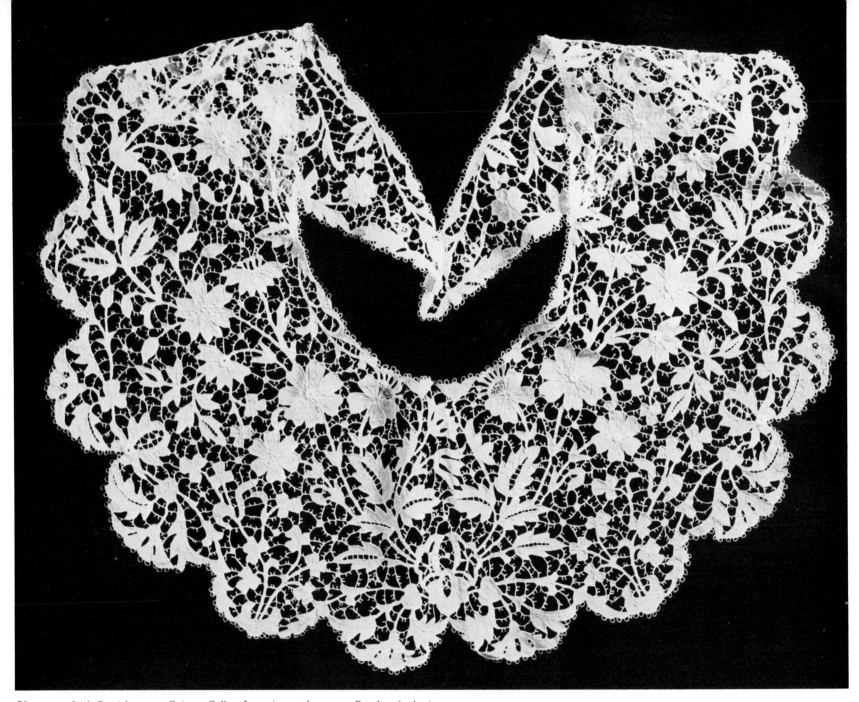

Plate 104 Irish Carrickmacross Guipure Collar. Late nineteenth century. Depth at back 16 cm.

Plate 105   Carrickmacross Appliqué Fan, with Mother-of-Pearl Sticks, c. 1870–90. Width of lace 23 cm.

Plate 106a   Needlepoint Border, perhaps Irish, c. 1870. Width 12.5 cm. The design is freely based on Venetian Point Lace.

Plate 106b   Youghal Needlepoint Lace, Irish, c. 1870. Width 16 cm.

extra layers of petals were often applied to the more prominent flowers which were nearly always roses.

The most prosperous period for hand-made lace in the nineteenth century was from about 1850 to 1870, but it ended with the Franco-Prussian War and the fall of the Second Empire. A gradual decline followed, while machine lace went forward triumphantly. From this time onwards there were to be no further major revivals for the hand industry.

In the last quarter of the century, lace for day-time wear was often heavier than any that had been fashionable ever since the seventeenth century, and unbleached or the darker écru shades were common. Brussels *Point Duchesse*, a rather heavy bobbin lace introduced in the middle of the century, silk Maltese in black or natural colour, woollen yak lace, Irish crochet and tape lace were all widely used. Much of the tape lace was made by amateurs as one of the popular craft hobbies of the period, and it was nearly all made from machine-woven tapes. The brides and fillings were needlepoint, in the tradition of seventeenth century tape lace, but almost invariably were far coarser. Heavy lace was often sewn over coloured material as a flat decoration. In contrast, for evening wear and for romantic tea gowns Point de Gaze and all the delicate laces were worn in profusion. Those who could afford them usually chose Brussels or Honiton appliqué for wedding veils and trimmings, but embroidered net was a popular and less expensive substitute.

Revivals of past styles also became very fashionable. Designs were copied and adapted from seventeenth and eighteenth century work, but they were often unsatisfactory. The little 'improvements' that designers could hardly

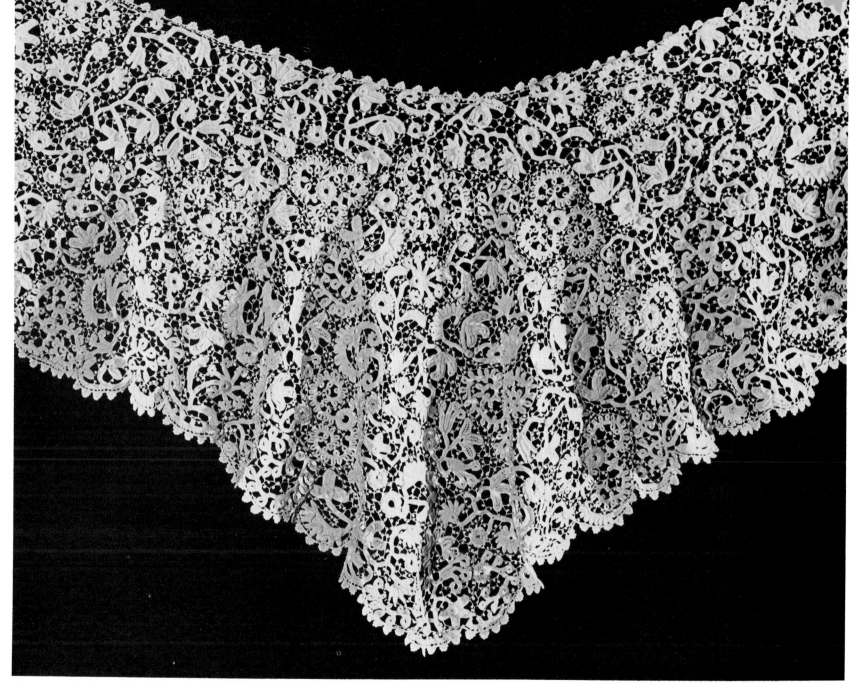

Plate 107   Irish Crochet Cape. Late nineteenth century. Greatest Depth 31 cm. The design is roughly based on Venetian Rose Point.

help making were inevitably more in the spirit of the nineteenth century than of the original designs, and much of the carefully made lace was disappointingly lifeless. Copies of sixteenth century reticella were more successful; their geometric patterns did not reflect the ideas of any particular period, but had developed naturally from the methods of the early lace-makers.

Venetian Rose Point was the most copied of all the old laces; it was popular in the 1870s, even more fashionable in the 1880s and to the end of the century, and was still being worn in the early years of this century. It was made in many different centres. Perhaps the greatest quantity came from Belgium, but some of the best copies were made on the island of Burano, near Venice. Lace had been made there in the great days of Venetian supremacy, but the craft had so declined by the early nineteenth century that only a little poor quality lace was being made. By the middle of the century even that had practically ceased. In 1872 the islanders were reduced to destitution by an extremely hard winter that froze the lagoons and made fishing, which was their only industry, impossible. The immediate distress was relieved from a charitable fund, and a lace school was founded to provide an alternative source of income. It was well managed and has prospered, with a very high standard of work being maintained. A collection of antique lace was made and many different styles were copied, but principally the various types of seventeenth century Venetian Point. Sometimes the work has a rather mechanical quality instead of the robust vigour of the original lace, but it never descended to the vulgarity and coarseness of some copies, the worst of which are a travesty of the beautiful seventeenth century design and work.

Real antique lace had enormous prestige amongst all the reproductions. It was more eagerly collected in the late nineteenth century than at any time before or since, but it was largely collected to be worn. It was cut up and reshaped for new fashions. Large pieces were patched together from fragments, and lace made of carefully bleached thread was tinted with tea or coffee to make sure it looked really antique.

For the first fourteen years of this century, until the First World War, lace remained as fashionable as it had been before 1900; there are records of the sales of some London stores showing that an even greater amount of lace was sold than ever before, but a great and growing proportion of it was machine-made. Making lace by hand, except in a few special circumstances, could not compete with other industries as a means of earning a living. The number of workers declined as the older ones died, and no new styles were created. 'Real' lace was still held in great esteem as a symbol of wealth and good taste, but came to be regarded romantically as a souvenir of the past – like Great Grandmother's wedding veil of 'priceless old Brussels'.

Needlepoint Lace

Some of the important laces made in this period have been described in the first part of this chapter to illustrate the trends in design and the general history of lace through the century. The following notes on the plates give some more technical details that may be interesting and help with identification.

The flounce of Alençon in Plate 96 is said to have been owned by the Empress Eugénie. It has very closely buttonholed cordonnets and a white horsehair carried round with the lowest one at the edge of the lace, and also round the outer petals of the rose in each spray of flowers and the tendrils and stems of the edging leaves. This was a feature of nineteenth century Alençon, to give extra crispness; it was not used in the earlier eighteenth century work. Some Alençon in the nineteenth century was partly made of cotton, which is surprising for such an expensive lace, but the réseau was always of linen thread for strength and firmness, and the highest quality was made entirely of linen. After 1860 Alençon was copied in Belgium, and from the late 1870s, also in Burano.

At first sight Brussels Point de Gaze and Alençon may look similar, which was of course the intention of the Brussels lace-makers, but there are unmistakable differences. The ground of Point de Gaze is very light and fragile; it was made of simple loops of buttonhole stitches in horizontal rows. The ground of Alençon is stronger; this was made, as in the eighteenth century, across the width of the lace, with twisted buttonhole stitches, and with an extra thread taken back across each row of loops before the next row was made. It was a more laborious ground to make, and wears better, but the very delicacy of the Point de Gaze ground does allow the design to appear almost to be hanging in space which gives a delightful airiness to the lace. The cordonnets of Point de Gaze were buttonholed over but not at all closely. The stitches were spaced out as in the rare Brussels needlepoint of the eighteenth century. In Alençon they touch each other tightly side by side. Horsehair was never used in Point de Gaze.

Plate 97 is of Brussels needlepoint appliqué on machine net, almost certainly using a French design. The needlepoint work is of the same character as that used for the motifs in Point de Gaze, but in this case it is particularly fine, and the applied relief petals and leaves are unusually varied and interesting. The normal Point de Gaze relief shown on Plate 99 consists of one, two or three extra layers of petals on the roses, but they have little variety of shape.

The panel of crochet, Plate 101, is French work. The subject and design are typical of the classical style of the first half of the nineteenth century. It is bolder and proportionately larger in scale than would have been probable in a late eighteenth century version of the same theme. It is more nearly derived from Roman art, instead of aiming at the refinement of the Greek. Designs of this type were used occasionally throughout the century for furnishing lace. Crochet work must be included among the lace-making techniques, but it only dates from the end of the eighteenth or early nineteenth century. It was developed from tambour embroidery, traditionally an eastern method that was introduced into Europe in the late seventeenth century. For this embroidery a small hook was used to pull loops of thread through the material and through each other. Crochet is the same process of making a chain of loops, but without a cloth ground. It became a popular form of fancy work in the early nineteenth century. At the same time fine knitting was also used as a new way of making lace, or at least an open lacy fabric that could be used as a substitute. When ingeniously designed and made of fine cotton thread it could be delicate and attractive (Plate 103).

Plate 102 is another classical design, but with an added touch of nineteenth century realism. It is probably also French, of about 1870, and

is carried out in the darned netting technique often used in the sixteenth and seventeenth centuries.

Lace-making in Ireland had an unusual history. There was no strong tradition for it in the country and when in the eighteenth century a patriotic group, known as the Dublin Society, tried to encourage both bobbin and needlepoint lace-making, they failed to establish a permanent industry. The first types of work to lead to substantial production were Carrickmacross, a cut work embroidery begun in the 1820s, and Limerick lace, founded in 1829, which consisted of both tambour and needle-run embroidery on machine net. There were two varieties of Carrickmacross, known as Carrickmacross Guipure, and Appliqué. For the first, the design was drawn on muslin or cambric, or on the paper over which the semi-transparent muslin was mounted. A thick thread was couched over the outlines, and then stitched to the muslin with close overcasting. Brides were worked with buttonholing and picots, where they would be needed to hold the pattern together. The work was then released from the backing paper and the spare muslin was cut away, close to the overcast outlines, leaving a solid design on an open ground, supported by brides (Plate 104). The second type was an appliqué on machine net; finer muslin could be used than for the guipure. The muslin was backed with net and the design outlined as before, the overcasting stitches passing through both the muslin and net. The unwanted muslin was carefully cut away, leaving the net as a continuous ground for the muslin pattern. Fillings were worked on parts of the ground and as centres for flowers and leaves (Plate 105). The earliest designs were said to have been copied from old Italian lace, but from

about 1850 naturalistic floral designs were popular. It is pretty lace, but neither type will wash satisfactorily. The edges of the pattern were only overcast, not buttonholed, and the muslin tends to shrink and pull away from the outline threads.

During the great potato famine of 1846 to 1848, and also in the later part of the century, lace-making was encouraged by philanthropic ladies and the Church, to help to relieve the great poverty. The production of Limerick and Carrickmacross was increased, and both were made in other parts of Ireland as well as in the original districts. Needlepoint lace-making was also established at various centres; the most important were Youghal, Kenmare and New Ross, where the work was taught in convents. Seventeenth century examples of Venetian Rose Point were studied and copied, and flat point lace was made both in designs based on seventeenth century styles and in contemporary designs (Plate 106a and b). Crochet work was introduced as a cottage industry in many districts during the famine period. It varied from fine to coarse, and from simple borders to large pieces, capes, dress trimmings and whole garments. The most elaborate designs were very free imitations of Venetian Rose Point, as in Plate 107.

The different centres of lace-making in Ireland were not all equally successful. Some of those started privately lasted only as long as their enthusiastic founders gave their time and energy to organizing and selling the work, but the convents had more permanent success and were managed on a sounder commercial basis. There were difficult periods, but the laces continued to be made in fluctuating quantities through the nineteenth and into the twentieth century.

Plate 108a   Burano copy of Venetian Rose Point. Width 8 cm.   Plate 108b   Burano copy of Venetian Rose Point. Width 6.5 cm.   Plate 108c   Burano copy of Argentan. Width 11.5 cm. All late nineteenth century needlepoint lace.

Reproductions of Venetian Point made on the island of Burano after 1872 included rich and important pieces as well as the usual adaptations for collars and other trimmings, and the intricate Point de Neige, not attempted in most centres, was also carefully copied there. Plate 109 is a good example of Burano Rose Point. It is elaborate and very well made, but as is so common with reproductions, the design lacks the power and conviction of the antique lace. The formal floral motifs seem to be manufactured from stock decorative fragments and have little sense of a direction of growth. The vigorously designed seventeenth century lace in Plate 38 has the qualities that this one lacks. Plate 106a shows a much simpler piece of nineteenth century Rose Point that succeeds better. Its design is so much further from the seventeenth century examples that it is not just a reproduction, but an original design with memories of a past style.

The two pieces of lace on Plate 110 are the only ones in this book that are not wholly European. One is a European example of a Near Eastern technique and the other, from Latin America, is based on a European tradition. The floral border is *Bibila* work, a needle-made knotted silk lace that probably originated in Turkey, but is also produced on the islands of Cyprus and Rhodes and around the eastern Mediterranean. It is often made in brightly coloured silks, but this border from Cyprus is a natural ivory colour. It is a typical design; the little plants, always with some work in relief, are made separately and lightly joined at only a few points.

The elegant panel of circular web-like designs in needle-weaving is from Paraguay, where it is known as *Nanduti*. The tradition was derived from Spain and Portugal, and dates back to the

Plate 109   Burano copy of Venetian Rose Point. Late nineteenth century. Complete panel 89×51 cm. This piece 38×29 cm.

Plate 110a   *'Nanduti', Needleweaving from Paraguay. Nineteenth century. Width 23 cm.*

Plate 110b   *'Bibila' Lace, Cyprus. Needle-made Knotted Lace. Late nineteenth or twentieth century. Width 7 cm.*

Plate 111 Brussels Veil, Bobbin-made Design Applied to Hand-made Ground, c. 1800–10. Complete veil 120 cm wide × 110 cm deep; Border 30 cm deep.

sixteenth century, but the early work was much stronger and heavier. The patterns were called *sols* and *ruedas* – suns and wheels. Similar work is done in other Latin American countries and in Tenerife, but not always with the lawn ground that was used as a basis for this lace, and not usually as fine. The beautiful variations of the design seem to be infinite.

Bobbin Lace

Plate 112 is of a Brussels stole, with bobbin-made appliqué on the vrai drochel ground, similar in period and style to the skirt of needle-point appliqué in Plate 93. The date of both would be about 1815 to 1825, when floral designs were beginning to be richer. They were still concentrated near the edges, which were often formed of a leaf motif, just as they had been at the end of the eighteenth century. The hand-made ground is very delicate and soft; the separately made narrow strips, about two centimetres wide, are joined horizontally in this piece.

All the lace on Plates 113 to 116 is silk lace of the types made at Chantilly, in districts near Paris, and at Caen and Bayeux in Normandy. Plate 113*b* and Plate 114 show the usual Blonde lace, with an extremely fine ground and the design in a thicker lustrous silk. It was mostly in the natural creamy colour from which it gets its name, but black Blonde was also made. The lace known as Chantilly was nearly all made of a mat black silk called 'grenadine' (Plates 115 and 116), but could be in natural-coloured silk (Plate 113*a*) or in linen or cotton. The clothwork of Chantilly was worked with the same threads as the ground, but outlined with a group of thicker threads. The main réseau of all this lace was the

Plate 112   Brussels Stole, Bobbin-made Appliqué on Hand-made Ground, c. 1820–25. Complete stole 209 × 46 cm.

Lille ground, a light hexagonal mesh made of only two twisted threads (Plate 132*b*). They also used the six-pointed star form, known as *fond chant* or *Point de Paris* (Plate 130*b*); the large mesh of the lower part of the flounce in Plate 114 is of this type. The deeply scalloped Blonde border, Plate 113*c*, is rather unusual. It includes some stiffening threads, which show as thicker white lines in the illustration; they are linen, closely wound with silk. This is probably a piece of the scalloped or pointed-edged Blonde that was worn, at the court of Napoleon I, standing up in a stiff frill from the sides and back of the low neckline of the ladies' classical dresses; it was a strange little fashion, by no means in the classical tradition.

From about 1805 to 1835 Blonde was extremely fashionable, but gradually during the late 1830s black Chantilly became the greater favourite, and after about 1840 copies, though of a lower quality, were being made in Belgium. Chantilly was very frequently used for large triangular or square shawls, worn over the wide-skirted dresses of about 1845 to 1870 as well as for small trimmings and fans (Plates 115 and 116). The large pieces were made in strips about nine centimetres wide and joined by a stitch known as *raccroc* stitch which is practically invisible. To the right of the bouquet, Plate 115, this has broken and the repair is visible; another join can just be seen passing through the top sprig, and there are two more between these. The joining is weaker than the mesh, so faults do occur on these lines after some wear. Chantilly lace was not as exclusive as Alençon as it was made in varying qualities, the finest being fit for the Empress Eugénie, but some for lesser mortals.

The Lille ground is always light but, made

Plate 113   White Silk Bobbin Lace.   a Chantilly Scarf, c. 1835. Width 19 cm; complete length 180 cm.   b Blonde Lace, c. 1830. Width 7 cm.   c Blonde Lace, with stiffening threads, c. 1805–15. Width 12 cm.

Plate 114   Flounce of Blonde Silk Bobbin Lace. Early nineteenth century. Width 44 cm.

Plate 115   Detail of Black Silk Chantilly Triangular Shawl, c. 1860. Shawl 294 cm wide, 150 cm deep, bouquet 50 cm high.

of linen or cotton, it can look more substantial than it does in the very fine silk of Blonde or Chantilly. Plate 117*a* is an actual piece of Lille lace, of characteristic early nineteenth century design, but rather more closely worked than usual. With it, Plate 117*b*, is a scarf of Buckinghamshire lace of about 1830 with the same ground, which in England is called the Buckinghamshire Point ground.

Plates 118, 119*b*, 120 and 121 are all of Honiton lace with patterns of bobbin sprigs. The eighteenth century style, with a réseau of the Brussels type of bobbin mesh, was not made after the early part of the nineteenth century. From about 1830 to 1860 the motifs were applied to machine net, as in Plate 118, for veils, flounces, berthas and general trimmings, and the appliqué was continued for wedding veils for the rest of the century. After about 1850 the smaller pieces of lace, for normal wear, began to be made of sprigs joined together in various ways. Plate 119*b* has bobbin-made plaited brides carried backwards and forwards between them, the extra threads for the brides being hooked into the edges of the clothwork. Plate 120 has a needlepoint mesh ground, and Plate 121 has rather carelessly made needlepoint bars.

The designs of the later Honiton lace were not always carefully or seriously considered. They tended to be jumbles of traditional shapes put together in a haphazard way, as in Plate 121, making an all-over texture rather than a design. The little collar, although simple, is a happier arrangement, and the sprigs themselves have more meaning. Some effort was made to produce well-designed lace for the 1851 Exhibition, and it succeeded in making a good impression. The workmanship was much admired, and for a short time Honiton became fashionable in

Plate 116   Black Silk Chantilly Fan, with Tortoise-shell sticks. Second half of the nineteenth century. Lace 14.5 cm deep.

Plate 117a   Lille Bobbin Lace Border, c. 1810. Width 6.5 cm.   Plate 117b   Scarf of Buckinghamshire Point Bobbin Lace. Early nineteenth century. Width 17 cm.

Plate 118   Honiton Bobbin Lace Appliqué on Machine Net, c. 1835–45. Width 27 cm.

France where some near copies were made during the 1850s. In the next twenty years or so, important exhibition pieces were produced with very pleasing naturalistic floral designs, but the majority of the workers continued to make the cheaper ordinary lace with jumbled patterns, and the industry had largely faded away by the end of the century.

Lace-making was revived in Malta in a very successful attempt to help the economic position. In 1833 Genoese workers were taken to Malta to teach bobbin lace techniques. Their work in the early nineteenth century was still more or less in the seventeenth century tradition, and the Maltese, who originally made reticella lace in the sixteenth century, had continued in a very limited way in that tradition. The newly founded Maltese bobbin lace was somewhat like the early Genoese lace, with its frequent use of the seed or wheat-grain form, and was also partly based on the formal geometric designs of reticella. It was nearly all made of black or cream silk, but cotton was used sometimes. The Maltese Cross was included in a great many of the designs.

This lace was shown at the Crystal Palace Exhibition with great success and became so fashionable that the industry expanded rapidly. Large capes, shawls and flounces were made as well as collars, handkerchiefs and other small pieces. The veil, Plate 122, is very fine and beautifully made, but most of the lace was of a more moderate quality, although quite effective; the wide border in Plate 123 is a typical example. It was not a very expensive lace, as it could be made comparatively quickly, and it remained popular to the end of the century. By then the quality had deteriorated and the lace was rather loose and coarse and was usually only

Plate 119a   Fichu with Buckinghamshire Point Border. Early nineteenth century. Lace 5.5 cm wide.

Plate 119b   Honiton Bobbin Lace Collar, with Bobbin-made Brides, c. 1860. 8.5 cm wide.

made for narrow borders, collars and cuffs.

After 1850 Maltese lace was copied all over Europe. It was produced for export at Le Puy and Mirecourt in France. In the East Midlands of England a version decorated with a great many picots, and known as Bedfordshire Maltese, was made rather coarsely in an effort to compete with cheap machine lace. It largely ousted the older and finer Buckinghamshire Point lace.

Such lace as had continued to be made in Italy into the nineteenth century was in the old traditions and had no influence on the fashionable lace designs of France and Belgium. It was only in the later part of the century, when reproductions of historical styles became fashionable, that Italy again came to some prominence, particularly with the Burano needlepoint. Genoa was the centre of another but less important revival, that of macramé. This is not strictly a lace, but originally a technique for knotting decorative fringes from the warp threads of woven linen. It was common in the sixteenth century, and some simple work was still being done at the beginning of the nineteenth century. Copies of more elaborate antique examples were made in Genoa in the 1840s and aroused fresh interest. From about 1860 the work became fashionable for separately made fringes used to trim garments and furnishings and was one of the many popular home crafts of the period. Plate 124 shows an elaborate Genoese example made of fine string.

Plate 120   Honiton Lace Bodice Trimming, with Needlepoint Ground. Late nineteenth century. Front opening 46 cm.

Plate 121   Detail of Honiton Bobbin Lace, with needle-made Brides. Late nineteenth century. Width 9.5 cm.

The modern kingdom of Belgium was created in 1831, but the lace-making traditions of Flanders continued, and Belgian bobbin lace maintained the great importance of the Flemish work. In the nineteenth century Valenciennes lace was produced mainly in Belgium, at Ypres and other towns, and formed a very considerable part of the country's lace industry. It was also made in quite large quantities at Bailleul, only ten miles from Ypres but just across the French frontier. The industry in Valenciennes itself never really recovered after the Revolution, and only a little of the lace was made there for a short time at the beginning of the century.

Eighteenth century Valenciennes had been made in the true straight lace technique, with exactly the same threads continuing all through the lace and forming the clothwork and the réseau, but a new method was introduced in the 1830s. A diamond-shaped mesh replaced the eighteenth century round mesh. It was still a strong ground as it was made of four thread plaits, but it was more open than the old réseau and so used fewer threads. To give the traditional solidity to the design extra threads had to be introduced for the clothwork; during the lace-making these were carried freely across the ground from one part of the solid pattern to the

next, and cut off afterwards. A close examination of the lace shows the groups of cut ends, which of course are never present in eighteenth century work. The new lace was somewhat quicker to make than the old and gave greater contrast between the density of the clothwork and the ground, which can be seen by comparing Plates 86*b* and 125. The designs of nineteenth century Valenciennes were usually rather uninteresting, with a very short repeat producing a monotonous and mechanical effect, but very large quantities of the lace were produced. Even the new type was slow and difficult to make, and very expensive, but no doubt its strength was

Plate 122   Black Silk Maltese Bobbin-made Veil. Mid nineteenth century. 77 × 41 cm.

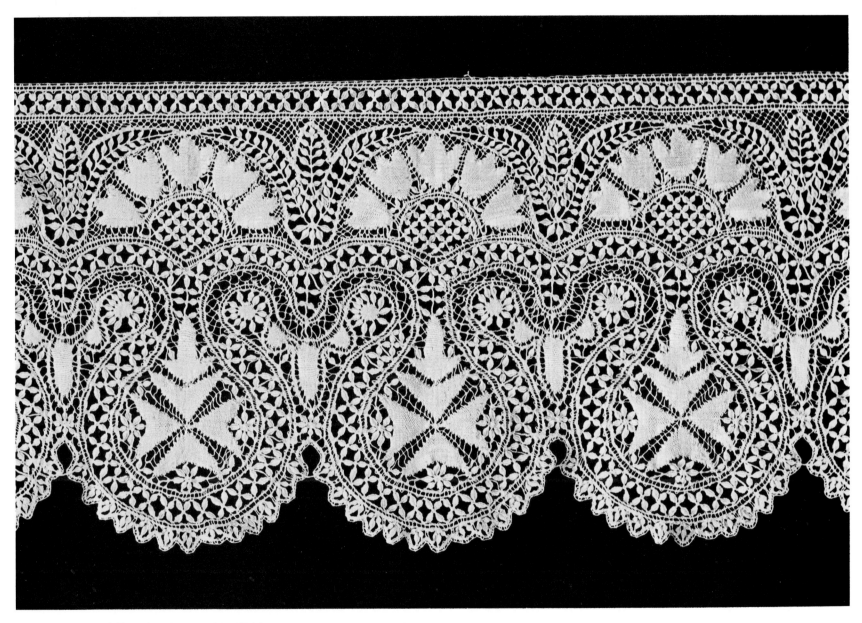

Plate 123   Cream Silk Maltese Lace, c. 1860. Width 24 cm.

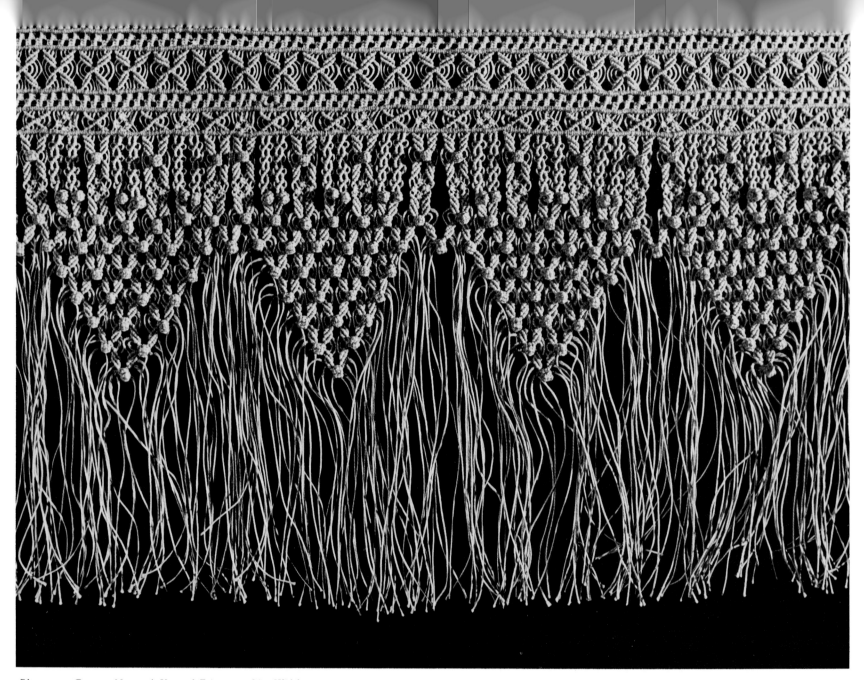

Plate 124   Genoese Macramé Knotted Fringe, c. 1860. Width 19 cm.

Plate 125   *Valenciennes Bobbin-made Borders. Second half of the nineteenth century. Widths 8.5 and 9 cm.*

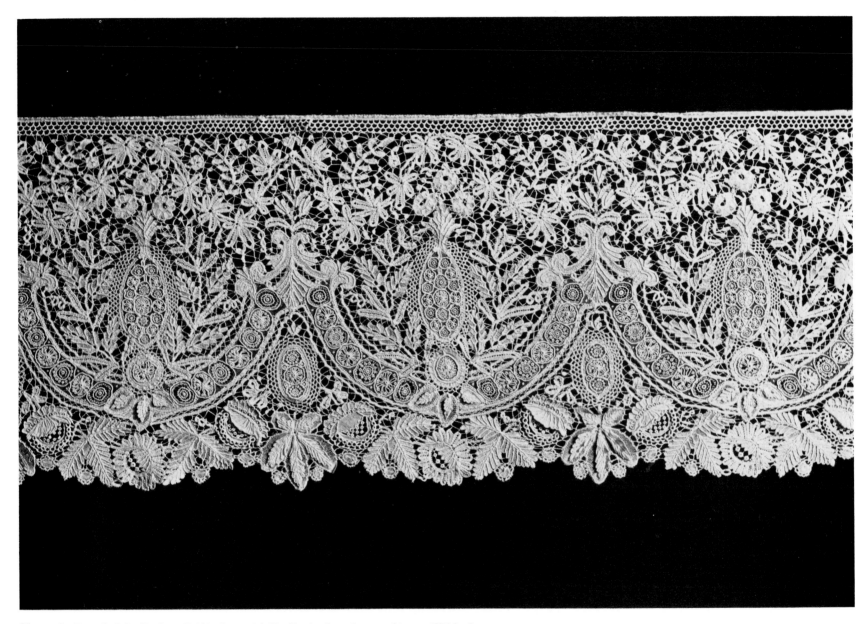

Plate 126   Brussels Point Duchesse Bobbin Lace, with Needlepoint Insertions, c. 1865–75. Width 28 cm.

Plate 127   Brussels Flounce with Bobbin-made Design and Brides, but Needle-made Réseau in the Panels. Made for Prince Leopold, fourth son of Queen Victoria. Second half of nineteenth century. Width 72 cm.

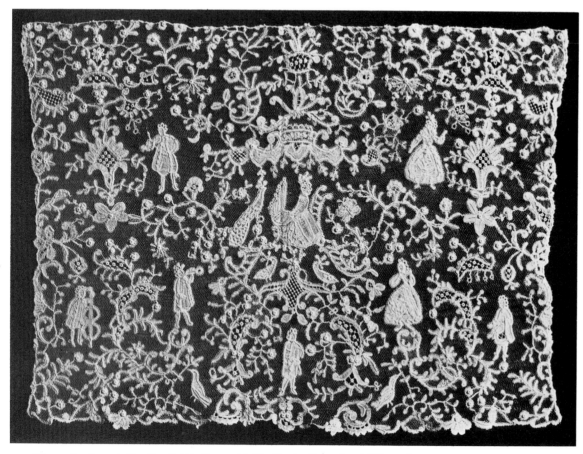

Plate 128 Brussels Rosaline Bobbin Lace, with Needlepoint Ground and Fillings. Design based on Point de France. Late nineteenth century. 34 × 25 cm.

by the same process as in the eighteenth and very early nineteenth century, but the later work was seldom as fine, and the cordonnets and raised lines on flowers and leaves were nearly always only a bundle of threads bound together at intervals, instead of being actually woven with the clothwork. As with other lace, designs in the middle of the century were rich, with large bouquets and trailing stems of flowers spreading over the ground. The deep flounce in Plate 100 is typical of the lace made for weddings in the 1860s and 1870s; it is of needlepoint appliqué, but similar designs were made with bobbin motifs. Brussels appliqué was nearly as popular as Chantilly for the large shawls and mantles fashionable from about 1845 to 1870. When these rather suddenly went out of fashion both industries suffered, but Brussels was not as seriously injured as Chantilly, as large wedding veils remained constantly in demand right through into the twentieth century. There was also a continuing desire for small pieces like handkerchiefs.

Point Duchesse was a new bobbin lace developed in Brussels around the middle of the century. It varied considerably in quality, but was on the whole coarser and cheaper than appliqué lace. The pattern of floral and other motifs was made by the usual method and joined by bobbin-made brides. It was strong and boldly effective and quickly became popular. The better qualities could be quite rich and often included panels of Point de Gaze or other needlepoint details to give variety of texture. Plate 126 shows such a piece; all the circular motifs and some of the flowers near the edge are needlepoint, and there is work in relief on these flowers and on the larger bobbin-made leaves. Some of the coarser and simpler Duchesse lace,

one reason for its popularity. It was freely used in the later part of the century for the decoration of underclothes, on which it would have to withstand constant washing.

The most interesting of the Belgian laces from the point of view of design were made in and around the city of Brussels. Appliqué was of major importance all through the century; it

could be of bobbin or needlepoint motifs, or of both sorts used together in the same design. Early examples on the hand-made ground have been described already, but from about 1835 it was nearly all on machine net, which was fine in the early part of the century though, for the average quality of lace, gradually became coarser. The bobbin motifs were basically made

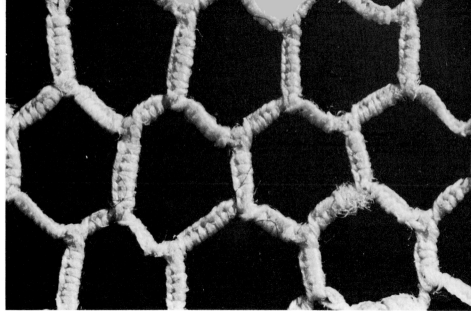

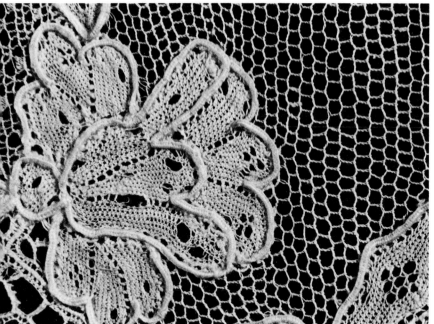

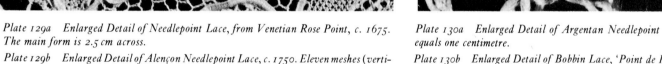

Plate 129a   Enlarged Detail of Needlepoint Lace, from Venetian Rose Point, c. 1675. The main form is 2.5 cm across.

Plate 129b   Enlarged Detail of Alençon Needlepoint Lace, c. 1750. Eleven meshes (vertical) equal one centimetre.

Plate 130a   Enlarged Detail of Argentan Needlepoint Réseau, c. 1750. Width of five meshes equals one centimetre.

Plate 130b   Enlarged Detail of Bobbin Lace, 'Point de Paris' or 'Fond Chant' Réseau, c. 1790. Six meshes (diagonal) equal one centimetre.

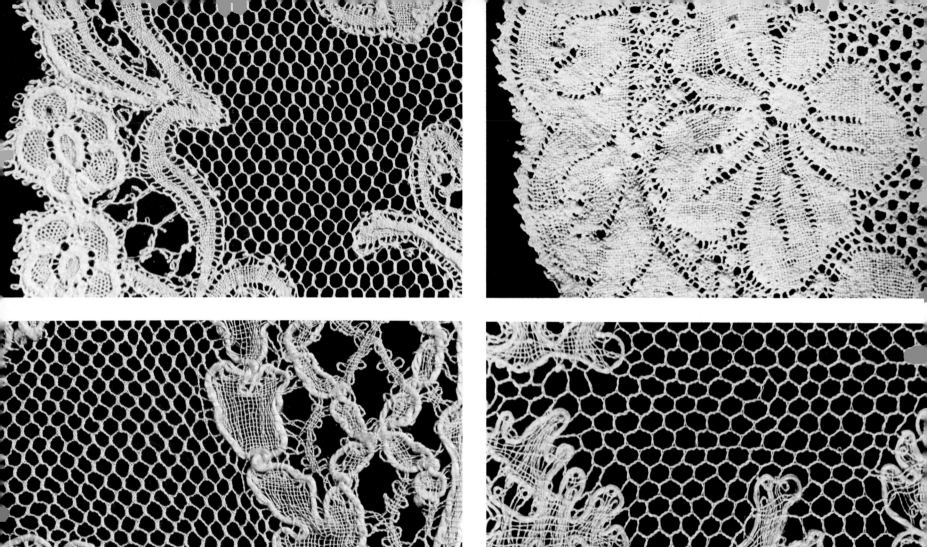

Plate 131a   Enlarged Detail of Brussels Bobbin Lace, c. 1780. Width of ten meshes equals one centimetre.

Plate 131b   Enlarged Detail of Mechlin Bobbin Lace, c. 1790. Width of eight meshes equals one centimetre.

Plate 132a   Enlarged Detail of Early Valenciennes Bobbin Lace, with 'Cinq Trous' Réseau, c. 1735. Maximum width of lace 3.5 cm.

Plate 132b   Enlarged Detail of Lille Bobbin Réseau, c. 1825. Width of seven meshes equals one centimetre.

without needlepoint additions, was made in Bruges. This lace continued successfully into the twentieth century and was very popular when heavy laces were fashionable from about 1875 to 1900.

The wide flounce of Brussels lace on Plate 127 is of unusual quality for nineteenth century lace. It was made by special order for Prince Leopold, fourth son of Queen Victoria, and includes his monogram of crossed 'L's, framed by the Garter with its motto, and surmounted by his coronet. The whole of the pattern and the bride ground are bobbin-made, but the mesh ground in the panels is needlepoint. The design mixes features characteristic of early and late eighteenth century styles; the general bold symmetrical arrangement and the bride ground are based on the earlier baroque forms, but the two-handled vases near the lower edge belong to the classical revival style of the last quarter of the eighteenth century.

The flounce is made of very fine linen thread, and there are several details of technique that are exceptional for its period. The cordonnets and raised lines enriching the motifs were woven with the clothwork, as they would have been in the eighteenth century, not just made of a group of threads as was usual during most of the nineteenth century. The needlepoint mesh is the Alençon réseau, with twisted buttonhole stitches and an extra thread carried back through the loops of each row, instead of the quicker and weaker Brussels Point de Gaze réseau. There are also an unusually large number of different delicate filling designs. Lace of this kind could not have been produced by workers used to the ordinary standards of this period. There must have been enough special orders to keep a few really highly skilled lace-makers in employment, and such orders would very naturally come to a great centre like Brussels.

Plate 128 is an amusing copy of a late seventeenth century Point de France cravat end, carried out in a fine Brussels bobbin lace called Rosaline, with a needlepoint réseau of the point de Gaze type and some needlepoint fillings and tiny rings in relief. The figures are a moderately close copy, but the surrounding ornament only just recalls the style of its distant ancestor.

Appendix – Collecting and Caring for Lace

I have collected antique lace for thirty-eight years, and have cherished and nursed back to life pieces that looked like dirty rags fit only for the dustbin. Possibly some of my experiences may be useful to collectors. It is a delightful hobby, and worth all the work to preserve and pass on beautiful things that are part of our history.

One could specialize in collecting one type of lace, but I very much recommend the idea of trying to acquire pieces that cover as much of the history as possible, so that the sequence of its styles can be followed. To find examples of lace all the way back to the sixteenth century sounds a daunting task, but it is not – the lace shown in this book is all from my own collection – it just happens bit by bit, as one works backwards from the nineteenth century. I remember the excitement of getting a little piece of late eighteenth century Alençon, because it opened the door into a new century. One can learn to identify types from scraps just as well as from important pieces, and it is much safer. All collectors must make some mistakes, but if possible it is better to make little ones. It really is not good to rush in and buy large important-looking pieces before one is sure of the difference between lace made by hand or by machine.

Searching for this all-important knowledge, I worried my eyes peering through a spyglass at a piece of machine-made lace, hoping to find out how it had been made by seeing if there were any irregularities, but it was all to no purpose. Beginning again, I tried studying enlarged photographs and diagrams, and it proved quite easy to recognize the simple structures that make up hand-made lace: the plaited threads and plain woven clothwork, and the little loops on the edge where the threads have been taken round the pins; and for needlepoint, the buttonhole stitches worked into each other and the buttonholed bars. If these clear forms are not found, the specimen is not hand-made. Machine lace looks more complicated, and some even has a muddled appearance when magnified, but it is not necessary to learn all the elaborate textures unless one wishes to collect machine lace. Large pieces, such as machine-made copies of Chantilly shawls, usually have a separately made and sewn on narrow looped edging to imitate the loops formed round the pins on the edge of bobbin lace, but such edgings have also been used sometimes to repair real bobbin lace, so they should be carefully examined. The clothwork of machine copies of bobbin lace frequently has a slightly ridged surface, instead of the even linen-like texture of bobbin work.

The question of the recognition of period style is more subtle; it does take time. Every design is different, yet all designs of any one period are imbued with a similar spirit. It can be useful to concentrate for a while on any period in which one is interested and study the designs of anything one can find, in museums or books, that was made at that time: furniture, pottery, silver, embroidery or anything else, as well as lace. Then go back half a century or so and see what led to those ideas, and forwards to see what came from them next. It is enthralling; one might finish up collecting pottery as well. I bought one of my first few pieces of lace at a Red Cross shop during the Second World War, knowing practically nothing about the subject; but as an art student I had learnt a little about the history of design, and thought the drawing of the flowers suggested seventeenth century work, but only considered it must be a traditional copying of the style. Imagine my joy, when I was told at the Victoria and Albert Museum that my piece was Italian lace of about the middle of the seventeenth century; it is the one on Plate 56a.

One important fact concerning style, which is a great help to the collector, is that practically speaking there were no deliberate copies until the second half of the nineteenth century. Some work, especially that made in provincial districts, might be a little old-fashioned at any time, but lace-makers of the mid eighteenth century simply did not make lace in the designs of the late seventeenth century. They all made lace that was fashionable in their own day; otherwise they could not have sold it. One has to be careful in watching for nineteenth century copies. Usually the later design has as strong a sense of the nineteenth century style as of the period it is copying, but mistakes certainly can be made. Be very wary about pieces that look lifeless or rigid. The copyist can never work with the vigour of an artist drawing freely in the style of his own period, which is as natural to him as his own signature.

Examination of the actual thread can be a help; no lace was made of cotton before the early nineteenth century, but copies of early work could be. It is not always possible to distinguish with certainty between linen and cotton thread without a microscope, but linen lace does feel cooler, smoother and firmer. Machine-spun thread was usually more tightly twisted than the traditional hand-spun thread. If one does get a nineteenth century copy by mistake, as most collectors do at some time, it is not a disaster, as one needs a few specimens in a representative collection, and if such a piece nestles for a while among earlier lace it will sooner or later be seen to be of a different breed.

The late nineteenth century fashion for wearing real antique lace created another danger for the collector, which particularly concerns the various Venetian Point laces. The brides of this lace never were as strong as the tightly made toilé, and when the linen is weakened with age, they easily break and let the lace fall apart. Being one of the most sought-after of all old laces, Venetian Rose Point fetched high prices, and it was commercially well worth while to rescue the fragments of the pattern, the formal flowers and leaves and miscellaneous bits of stem, and reconstruct a lace that was really a patchwork. The new brides holding it all together might be buttonholed as in the original lace, or were sometimes bobbin-made, as much of this work was done by Devonshire lace-makers accustomed to bobbin work.

These reconstructions may still be rich in texture, but they are of no value to the collector, as they have lost the form of the original design. In the better examples some fairly large pieces of lace may remain intact, but with nasty jerks in the lines where unfortunate joins have been made. The worst pieces are an absolute jumble of scraps, taken from different pieces of lace of varying qualities. These are very easy to distinguish, as they have no form at all. The design of the original seventeenth century Gros Point and Rose Point is always strong and definite with firmly drawn branches growing forward in powerful scrolls, and the principal forms repeat as they were intended to do, often with variations of detail but not in the broad outlines that were worked, for each repeat, over the same parchment.

This patching up of scraps is quite different from good repair work, which is often essential for the preservation of damaged lace, and in which broken brides would be replaced or joined in their correct position, leaving the design exactly as it was made. Patched lace was often reconstructed in the shapes of fashionable collars and other trimmings unknown in the seventeenth century. Perfectly good unaltered lace of all types was also frequently cut into nineteenth century shapes. These cannot necessarily all be rejected, and many will be found in museums, but it is infinitely better to have lace in its original shape. In all cases the design will show any changes that have been made. Forms were arranged to be well balanced within their borders; no curving stem was intended to disappear over the edge and reappear a little further along, or just get completely lost. Flowers and other motifs were never chopped in half along an arbitrary line.

I have often been asked where I have bought my lace, and there is no simple answer. I try to be on the watch always and everywhere. If one sees an interesting looking end hanging over a shelf or peeping out of a pot, it is worthwhile investigating, but of course, usually it is nothing special. The impossible can happen, and very occasionally it does. I bought the Rose Point collar, on Plate 41, from a lady who had got it at a jumble sale for sixpence. She asked me fifteen shillings for it, and we were both very pleased.

Lace can fairly often be found at markets; not magnificent pieces, but sometimes interesting ones. There are a few dealers in such places who specialize in textiles and usually have some lace, but most dealers know very little about it and only get pieces accidentally among other things, so prices vary enormously. Lace is not very widely collected, and compared with most antiques it is still cheap, but it is growing in popularity, and correspondingly the prices are rising.

Some of the best auctioneers have periodic sales of textiles, including embroideries and sometimes costume and lace, and more important pieces can be expected at these. It is essential to view the lace beforehand, as it is impossible to assess the condition and quality as it is actually being sold. Most lots are made up of several pieces, or sometimes a large bundle; only the more valuable specimens are sold separately. A great deal can be learnt at both views and auctions.

Occasionally one is lucky enough to buy a piece of lace, clean and in good condition, that can go straight into one's collection, but far more often it needs mending and washing. It is better to do the necessary mending first, because if there is a tear or break, the next threads are under strain and would probably break during the washing. It has always been difficult to find needles or thread fine enough for most of the work, and it is rapidly becoming even more difficult. Not many years ago number 150 cotton was freely available, but now number 60 seems to be the finest in ordinary shops. For most repairs this is far too thick; it looks like rope in fine lace, and makes one realize just how fine some lace is. The best thing now may be to draw threads from organdie or silk organza, unless one has the good fortune to find some left-over hanks of fine linen or cotton lace thread in one of the old lace-making districts. I have used thread from old lace bobbins and found tiny reels of number 200 and 250 cotton, and very fine needles, in a Victorian work-box, and I have divided number 150 crochet cotton into three strands. It has practically become another branch of collecting. The finest needles now obtainable, as far as I know, are beading needles, very long and pliable and not really suitable for the work, but better than coarse needles. Linen gradually becomes brittle with age, and a coarse or blunt needle can very easily break the thread instead of parting the fibres.

I can only describe methods I have used myself for mending and washing, but I do wish to say that they are very ordinary domestic methods, not museum conservation procedure. It is possible to get advice from museums if one wishes.

Every mending problem is different; one just has to consider the best possible method for each particular specimen. Working with a needle on bobbin lace cannot exactly replace the lost work, but if threads are suitably fine, and carried in the same direction as the original ones, they are inconspicuous. If the damage is reasonably close to a piece of clothwork, it is advisable to take the mending thread forward to it before turning back to cross the damage again. In any case it is unwise to try to work so neatly that one's threads hardly overlap the remaining lace. Many very dainty professional nineteenth cen-

tury repairs, particularly on machine net grounds, had practically no overlap and have broken away again from the edges.

The most important thing of all is to lay the lace out smoothly, see that it is not distorted, and only join points that were originally together. If there is a missing piece, it is disastrous to draw the edges together and pull the lace out of shape. Somehow the missing area must be remade, with brides, or a buttonhole stitched mesh, or a sort of needleweaving – whatever fits best. Rose Point is one of the easiest laces to repair; the necessary work is nearly always to replace lost brides, which can be made and buttonholed as they were at the beginning. Always do this work from the back of the lace. The brides should be attached to the edges of the toilé and pass behind the raised work without touching it. If the new brides clutch the raised edges, as they often do when they have been worked from the front, they look very ugly and clumsy. When the lace was originally made all the work was done from the front, over the parchment, but the brides were made before the raised work was added as the final stage.

Quite often repair work has to begin with the tedious and rather distressing job of unpicking previous thoughtless mending that has muddled the design by joining up the wrong parts. I am not referring to the lace that has been reconstructed from fragments of Venetian Point – that is beyond repair – but to lace that has simply been badly mended. With care and patience the design can be sorted out by looking at other repeats or the other half of a symmetrical layout, or just following the direction of growth of plant forms. A slightly clumsy mend may be best left alone if it does not interfere with the design, as the

unpicking itself can easily do some damage.

Dirty lace gives me little joy, except in anticipation of the effect of cleaning. The delicate beauty seems to be insulted by dirt and grease, but much of the lace I have acquired has been dirty, and some horribly dirty, for so many people are afraid to wash it. This should be done with the greatest care, and only when really necessary, as inevitably the process must wear the fabric to some degree.

I use water that has been boiled, cooled, and then poured gently into another vessel, leaving any cloudy sediment behind, and plain White Windsor soap, rubbed into the water to make suds, but never, never, rubbed on the lace. All the vessels needed should be large enough to allow the lace to float freely. I do not recommend any form of bleaching; they all rot the fibres, and I would rather ignore such persistent stains as withstand washing than shorten the life of my lace.

First the lace is soaked for an hour or two in warm soapy water; if it is very dirty this will become yellowish, and will need changing for a second soak. It can be left entirely still; the less movement the better. If the lace has been dyed in tea or coffee, which unfortunately was often done in the late nineteenth century, quite a lot of the colour will soak out, and the water will be a pinkish brown. Every time the lace is moved from one water to the next it should be lifted from underneath, to support its weight, held still to drip a little, and then lowered into the new water. This is especially important for the heavier old laces, which hold so much water that the weakened threads cannot support the weight unaided. After soaking, the lace is rinsed, put into new suds, and then very slowly heated, without being disturbed at all, until the water just simmers. This can be continued for a time if it is necessary. The simmering water percolates through the lace far more gently than any sort of rubbing or swishing about, but of course, only linen or cotton can be taken to this temperature. For white or cream silk lace the water should be no hotter than is quite comfortable for the hand, and for coloured silk or metal lace only dry cleaning liquids can be used.

When sufficiently cool, the lace can be lifted out and placed in two or three rinsing waters, and then on to a towel and left just as it is until most of the water has soaked away. When it is dry enough not to cling together, it can be spread carefully on dry towels under which there are several layers of paper that help to take the moisture and also prevent any stain, for example from a wood surface, from coming through the towels to the lace. When it is dry, or with only a hint of dampness, gentle ironing on the back will straighten and shape the lace,

and raised work will need lifting from the front. In spite of all the care taken, there may then be a few minor repairs to make.

I once had a disaster; it is a cautionary tale. I bought a very beautiful large early nineteenth century stole of Brussels bobbin appliqué on a hand-made ground. The design was of wheatears forming diagonal stripes about eight centimetres apart, with hundreds of tiny rings powdering all the ground between them, and with deep borders of oak branches at the ends and narrower ones down the long sides. It was not very dirty, but nevertheless not clean, and I decided to wash it. There were no holes to mend – only the tips of a few leaves were coming loose and I thought I could sew them down later – so I proceeded with the washing as I have described. When the water was quite hot I peeped in to see that all was well, and to my horror, saw what looked like lace seaweed float-

ing in the soapy water, its loose ends waving gently just below the surface, and the little rings swimming all around in their hundreds. Rescue operations involved the family, and the whole 'lace soup', as it was promptly christened, was poured through a large colander, lined with muslin, to save the little rings. Several weeks later they were all sewn back, and all the seaweed was innocently lying in its well-ordered classical stripes and borders.

There is a moral to the tale. If only I had stitched back the loose ends before thinking of washing the lace, I should have discovered that the original sewing thread, finer than my sample of number 350 linen, was so weakened and so fragile that it would be wiser not to risk the washing – far better to leave it as it was, though just a little dirty!

Glossary

Appliqué Needlepoint or bobbin lace motifs sewn on to a continuous ground of either bobbin or machine-made net.

Argentella A rich eighteenth century needlepoint lace that has a larger proportion than usual of elaborate fillings, or a complete ground of one of the designs that were normally used as fillings. It is a variant of Point d'Argentan lace, probably made both in France and in Venice, copying the French style in the early eighteenth century.

Bars See *brides*.

Blonde lace A French silk bobbin-made lace, most fashionable from about 1805 to 1835. It was usually made of natural cream-coloured silk, the réseau of a very fine thread, and the design of a thicker lustrous silk.

Bobbin lace or *pillow lace* Lace made by twisting, crossing and plaiting threads round and between pins that control the design. The threads are carried on lace bobbins, and the work is supported on a pillow.

Bone lace A name often used for bobbin lace in England in the sixteenth century. The bobbins used may have been made of bone, or actual small bones may have been used as bobbins.

Brides or *bars* The plaits in bobbin lace, or the buttonholed threads in needlepoint lace, that connect the different parts of the pattern together. They are only necessary in lace that has no background mesh to support the pattern. Brides are often decorated with little knots, or picots, and are then called *brides picotées*.

Bride tortillée A needlepoint ground used in the second half of the eighteenth and in the nineteenth century, at Alençon and Argentan. It was a hexagonal mesh, with the sides of the hexagons whipped over with a single thread, instead of being buttonholed over as in the true Argentan ground.

Buratto Netting with an embroidered or darned-in pattern, similar to lacis, but the buratto netting is made by twisting threads instead of knotting them.

Cartisane lace Early lace including narrow strips of parchment covered with silk, or gold or silver thread.

Clothwork The solid part of bobbin lace that resembles plain weaving in appearance, sometimes also used for the solid areas of needlepoint lace. See also *toilé*.

Collar Lace The name given to the edging lace with rounded scallops that was used to decorate collars from about 1625 to a little after the middle of the century. It can refer to either needlepoint or bobbin lace.

Col Rabat The type of collar worn by gentlemen from about 1655 to about 1670 or 1680.

It was square-fronted, and rich examples were trimmed with Rose Point.

Coralline Point One of the needlepoint laces made in Venice at the end of the seventeenth century and early in the eighteenth century. It has small meandering designs, said to have been based on the branching forms of coral.

Cordonnet A raised outline to the pattern of needle-made or bobbin lace, made of thicker thread or of a group of threads. In needlepoint lace these were buttonholed over.

Cravat In about 1670 to 1680, the cravat replaced the col rabat as the fashionable neckwear for men. It was a long strip of fine linen, usually with lace ends, that was twisted round the neck and tied at the front.

Dentelle (French) Lace. From *dent*, a tooth. In the sixteenth century *passement dentelé* described the early lace edgings with tooth-like points.

Droschel or *drochel* or *vrai drochel* Hand-made bobbin ground for Brussels appliqué lace. After about 1830, machine-made net was normally used instead of hand-made.

Engageantes Shaped sleeve ruffles, worn by ladies from about 1690 to about 1780.

Fil continu See *straight lace*.

Filet See *lacis*.

Fillings, modes or *à jours* The decorative openwork used in enclosed areas of both needlepoint and bobbin lace designs, in contrast with the normal plainer ground mesh or the brides.

Flat Point or *Point Plat*   Needlepoint lace with no extra work in relief. These terms are used especially for the flat seventeenth century Venetian lace to distinguish it from the richer lace made there at the same period that is famous for its raised work.

Fond Chant or *Point de Paris*   A bobbin-made ground in which the mesh forms six pointed star-like shapes.

Gimp   A thick thread used to outline the pattern in bobbin lace.

Gros Point   See under *Rose Point*.

Guipure   Most commonly used for heavy or moderately heavy lace in which the parts of the pattern are joined by brides, not by a mesh. In the sixteenth and seventeenth centuries the word meant a thick thread covered with silk or metal wire, and gold and silver lace was also referred to as guipure. In the nineteenth century the word was used frequently and loosely, with varied meanings, so perhaps it is best to avoid it if possible.

Holy or *Hollie Point*   English needlepoint lace used especially to trim christening clothes, and made in the same way as the fillings of Venetian Point Lace.

Kant   (Dutch) Lace.

Lacis or *filet*   Knotted netting, with a pattern darned into it.

Lappets   Two long, narrow pieces of lace hanging from a lady's head-dress, fashionable for formal occasions from the late seventeenth century, through the eighteenth century, and still worn occasionally in the nineteenth century.

Macramé   Knotted fringe. Originally made as a decorative finish from the warp threads of woven linen, the craft was revived in the nineteenth century in Genoa and became popular for separately made fringes.

Mezzo punto or *tape lace*   The pattern of this lace is formed from a continuous braid or tape. In early specimens this was bobbin-made, but in nineteenth and twentieth century pieces the tape is almost invariably machine-made. The ground-work of mesh or brides and the fillings are needle-made.

Mixed lace   Lace made partly with the needle and partly with bobbins; for example, needle-point floral designs joined by a bobbin-made ground.

Modes   See *fillings*.

Needlepoint lace   Lace made with needle and thread, over a design drawn on parchment.

Pieced lace   Bobbin lace in which the pattern is worked first and the ground, or brides or mesh, is worked round the completed pattern.

Pillow lace   See *bobbin lace*.

Plaited lace   Bobbin lace made principally of plaited threads which are interwoven as they cross each other, and with only small areas of clothwork.

Point   (French) Stitch.

Point d'Angleterre   This is not at all what the name suggests. It is a very fine bobbin lace made in Brussels during the eighteenth century. It was in great demand in England, but during some parts of the century its import was forbidden, and it was widely smuggled. The name was probably used to help the pretence that it had been made in England. Devonshire lace-makers did use the same technique, but their lace was less sophisticated.

Point d'Espagne   Gold and silver lace was usually called Point d'Espagne in France during the sixteenth and seventeenth centuries when it was much used by the wealthy. Colbert encouraged its making in France in the second half of the seventeenth century, but it still seems to have been known as Point d'Espagne.

Point de France   Needlepoint lace made in France, under royal patronage, from 1665 until the beginning of the eighteenth century when Alençon and Argentan gradually replaced it as the more fashionable laces. Louis XIV's minister Colbert was responsible for the introduction of Point de France, and Louis XIV himself gave it its name.

Point de Gaze   A nineteenth century needlepoint lace made in Brussels from about the middle of the century. The designs are usually of naturalistic sprays and swags of flowers, sometimes with separate layers of petals in relief.

Point de Neige   See under *Rose Point*.

Point lace   Logically this should only refer to needle-made lace, but it has often been used to suggest fine quality in bobbin laces, such as 'Buckinghamshire Point'. It is therefore better to use the term 'needlepoint lace' when meaning lace made with the needle.

Point Noué   Button hole stitch.

Point Plat See *Flat Point*.

Potten Kant Bobbin Lace with designs using a symmetrical vase of flowers as the principal motif, made in the seventeenth and eighteenth centuries, mainly in and around Antwerp.

Punto (Italian) Stitch.

Punto a Festone Buttonhole stitch.

Punto a Groppo or *Punto Avorio* Punto in Aria with a very closely worked toilé of needle-made knots (*groppo:* a knot), supposed to look like the surface of ivory (*avorio:* ivory).

Punto in Aria Literally – stitch in the air. Needlepoint lace of the sixteenth and early seventeenth centuries constructed of linen thread, or occasionally of silk, over a parchment design without a foundation of woven linen or netting. Most commonly used for pointed edging lace, but can refer to straight-sided lace constructed in the same way and during the same period.

Punto Tagliato Cut linen work.

Réseau The mesh ground of either needle-point or bobbin lace.

Reticella Needlepoint lace constructed in rectangular spaces in cut linen. The designs are mainly geometric.

Rose Point Needlepoint lace with work in relief. 'Rose' here simply means raised.

'Rose Point' is used mainly for the very rich laces, with elaborate raised work, that were made in Venice from about 1650 to about 1700, and for copies of these laces. 'Raised Venetian Point' is a useful alternative name for the whole group of laces, as the term Rose Point is often used specifically for the intermediate style of this lace that was made from about 1660 to about 1695, between the early Gros Point and the late Point de Neige.

Gros Point The earliest form, with bold scrolling patterns and strong relief, made from the middle of the seventeenth century to about 1665. *Gros*, meaning large, only refers to the scale of the designs, not to any coarseness of thread or workmanship. The designs were gradually reduced in scale as time went on and the word *gros* was no longer applicable.

Rose Point The intermediate style has no other name than Rose Point. Designs were of a very similar nature but became more elaborate as the scale was reduced. Rose Point was made from about 1660 to 1690 or 1695. There were no sudden changes, and types overlap.

Point de Neige The latest of the Rose Point laces, with much smaller versions of the early designs and very elaborate but dainty relief, light enough to resemble a fall of snow-flakes; hence the name. It was made from about 1685 to 1700 or a few years later.

Spanish Point Needlepoint lace, with work in relief, made in Spain from about 1660 to about 1715. It was somewhat similar to Venetian Rose Point, but with less well controlled and less magnificent designs. 'Spanish Point' can mean also the gold and silver lace made in Spain and exported to other countries, but the French name 'Point d'Espagne' was more frequently used for this.

Straight lace or *fil continu* Bobbin lace in which the same threads are used right through the lace to form the solid clothwork, the mesh ground and the fillings, as the work proceeds. In the finished lace the threads lie more or less parallel with the sides of the lace, or at right angles to them.

Tape lace See *mezzo punto*.

Tela tirata Drawn thread work.

Toilé The close textured, more solid part of either needlepoint or bobbin lace. 'Clothwork' means the same, but is used most frequently for the solid part of bobbin lace.

Trolle or *trolly* Thick outlining thread in bobbin lace. Gimp.

Venetian Point Needlepoint lace, with or without relief work, made in Venice. It usually refers to that made between about 1650 and 1700. See also under *Rose Point*.

Vrai drochel See *droschel*.

Bibliography

Bath, Virginia Churchill. *Lace*. Cassell & Collier Macmillan, London, 1974.

Cole, Alan S. *Ancient Needlepoint and Pillow Lace*. Arundel Society, London, 1875.

Jackson, Mrs F. Nevill. *History of Hand-Made Lace*, 1900.

Jourdain, M. *Old Lace: A Handbook for Collectors*. B. T. Batsford, London, 1908.

Meulen-Nulle, L. W. van der. *Lace*. The Merlin Press, London, 1963.

Palliser, Mrs Bury. *History of Lace*. Sampson, Low, Son & Marston, London, 1865. Fourth edition, edited by M. Jourdain and A. Dryden, Sampson Low & Co., London, 1902.

Pollen, Mrs J. Hungerford. *Seven Centuries of Lace*. William Heinemann, London and the Macmillan Company, New York, 1908.

Trendell, P. G. *Guide to the Collection of Lace*, Victoria and Albert Museum. H.M.S.O., London, 1930.

Wardle, Patricia. *Victorian Lace*. Herbert Jenkins Ltd, London, 1968.

Index